FOUR DAYS

THE HISTORICAL RECORD

OF THE DEATH

OF PRESIDENT KENNEDY

compiled by

UNITED PRESS INTERNATIONAL

and

AMERICAN HERITAGE MAGAZINE

Published by AMERICAN HERITAGE PUBLISHING CO., INC.

Introduction

By BRUCE CATTON

Senior Editor of AMERICAN HERITAGE *Magazine*

What John F. Kennedy left us was most of all an attitude. To put it in the simplest terms, he looked ahead. He knew no more than anyone else what the future was going to be like, but he did know that that was where we ought to be looking. Only to a limited extent are we prisoners of the past. The future sets us free. It is our escape hatch. We can shape it to our liking, and we had better start thinking about how we would like it.

It was time for us to take that attitude, because we thought we were growing old. We had lived through hard experiences and we were tired, and out of our weariness came caution, suspicion, and the crippling desire to play it safe. We became so worried about what we had to lose that we never began to think about what was still to be gained, and sometimes it looked as if we were becoming a nation of fuddy-duddies. The world was moving faster than ever before and we were beginning to regret that it was moving at all because we were afraid where it might take us.

But President Kennedy personified youth and vigor—and perhaps it was symbolic that both his friends and his foes picked up his Boston accent and began to say "vigah." He went about hatless, he liked to mingle with crowds and shake the hands of all and sundry, for recreation he played touch football, and for rest he sat in an old-fashioned rocking chair as if in sly mockery of his own exuberance. He seemed to think that things like music and painting and literature were essential parts of American life and that it was worthwhile to know what the musicians and artists and writers were doing. Whatever he did was done with zest, as if youth were for the first time touching life and finding it exciting.

With all of this there was a cool maturity of outlook. By itself, vigor is not enough. Courage is needed also, and when youth has courage it acquires composure. In the most perilous moments President Kennedy kept his poise. He challenged the power of darkness at least once, and during the hours when his hand had to stay close to the fateful trigger he was composed and unafraid. Once in a great while a nation, like a man, has to be ready to spend itself utterly for some value that means more than survival itself means. President Kennedy led us through such a time, and we began to see that the power of darkness is perhaps not quite as strong as we had supposed—and that even if it were, there is something else that matters much more.

It was his attitude that made the difference. Performance can be adjudged in various ways, and we have plenty of time to appraise the value or the lack of value of the concrete achievements of the Kennedy Administration. The President who called on us to stop thinking about what our country could do for us and to think instead about what we could do for our country may or may not have given us specific programs that would embody that ideal in actual practice; the point is that he wrenched us out of ourselves and compelled us to meditate about the whole that is greater than the sum of its parts. From the beginning, the whole of our American experiment has been made up of an infinite number of aspirations and unremembered bits of heroism, devotion, and hope, lodged in the hearts of innumerable separate Americans. When all of these are brought together, the nation goes forward.

That, in the last analysis, is the faith America has wanted to live by. We are always uneasy when we find ourselves keeping our noblest ideals in mothballs, carefully shielded from contact with the workaday world; deep in our hearts we know that we are supposed to take them out and work for them even if contact with harsh reality occasionally knocks chips off of them here and there. Whether this man knew the best ways to put our ideals into practical use is a secondary consideration now. He did think that we ought to try our best to do something about them, and that belief his death did not take away from us, because we came to share in it.

We turned some sort of corner in the last few years. Almost without our knowing it, one era came to an end and a new one began. The change had little to do with formal acts of government—with specific programs, bits of legislation, or exercises of presidential power. It reflected a change in the times themselves. For a whole generation we had had to face terrible immediate problems—depression, war, cold war, the infinite destructive power of the nuclear mystery that we knew how to release but did not quite know how to control. Then came a breathing spell, a faint but definite easing of the tensions. Almost for the first moment in our lifetimes we began to look ahead once more and to realize that it was not only possible but imperative to think about the limitless future rather than about the mere problem of warding off disaster.

President Kennedy came to symbolize that moment of change, not because he caused it but because he fitted into it; not because of what he did but simply because of what he was. He might almost have been speaking from Shakespeare's text, telling us that being ready is what really matters—being ready to meet any challenge, to assume any responsibility, to lose fear for ourselves in an abiding concern for the common good. The four harrowing days that began on November 22, 1963, brought us face to face with the future. What happens next is up to us. The readiness is all.

That is why those four days are worth re-examining. We relive that time of tragedy less to commemorate a departed President than to dedicate ourselves. When the army bugler sent the haunting notes of "Taps" across that grave in Arlington Cemetery he sounded a long goodbye and a commitment to eternal rest for John F. Kennedy. For all the rest of us, that was the trumpet of dawn itself.

FRIDAY

22

NOV. 1963

Friday dawned misty, unpromising for a day to be spent seeing the people and politicking. Then the skies cleared and the weather grew balmy. The President was in Texas primarily for political reasons—to help heal a rift in his party there and to hold the state for the Democrats in 1964—and he was undoubtedly pleased to find the weather co-operating. People have a natural reluctance to stand in the rain to watch a motorcade of closed cars go by, even if one of them is carrying the President of the United States.

It had, in fact, been a political week. On Monday, November 18, he spoke to audiences in Tampa and Miami Beach. That night he flew back to Washington for a two-day interlude of official business. At a White House reception for the Justices of the Supreme Court, the First Lady returned to the social scene for the first time since the death of her infant son in August. On Thursday, the President and his wife flew to Texas.

There were warnings that the President's reception might be chilly. Of late, Texas had been in an unfriendly mood toward the Administration. Partly, this flowed from the civil rights issue; partly it was aroused by militant right-wing groups. Vice President Lyndon Johnson, himself a Texan, was frequently vilified. Ambassador to the United Nations Adlai Stevenson had recently been spat upon and hit with a picket's sign in Dallas. Placards were being distributed bearing the President's picture and a legend: *Wanted for Treason.*

Yet Thursday's receptions in San Antonio, Houston, and Fort Worth were warm and enthusiastic. The First Lady was a great hit with the crowds. Little wonder that John F. Kennedy began this day, Friday, with relaxed confidence. Everything was obviously going well.

The President's day began in intimate contact
with smiling, friendly Texans outside his
hotel. There was disappointment that the First
Lady was not with him. "Mrs. Kennedy is
busy organizing herself," he explained. "It
takes a little longer, you know,
but then she looks so much better than we do."

A cheerful morning in Fort Worth

At 8:45 A.M. President Kennedy emerged from his hotel in Fort Worth and strode across the street to greet a crowd waiting for him in a parking lot. Then he returned to the hotel to speak at a Chamber of Commerce breakfast. Jacqueline Kennedy, lovely in a pink suit and pillbox hat, made a late entrance. The President was in a joking mood; he recalled that on a state visit to France two years before he introduced himself as "the man who had accompanied Mrs. Kennedy to Paris. I'm getting somewhat that same sensation as I travel around Texas. Nobody wonders what Lyndon and I wear." His speech dealt with Fort Worth's role in the nation's defense effort: "this is a very dangerous and uncertain world," he said. Then the party hurried to the airport for the short flight to Dallas, where the President was to address a luncheon. Again, defense was to be his topic, but he also planned to speak out against the "voices preaching . . . that vituperation is as good as victory and that peace is a sign of weakness."

At right, Texas Governor John Connally, Mrs. Lyndon Johnson, Vice President Johnson, and the President bow their heads in prayer at the Chamber of Commerce breakfast.

Welcome in Dallas

At 11:37 the big presidential jet, Air Force One, touched down at Dallas' Love Field. Several thousand enthusiastic, good-natured Texans cheered as the Kennedys appeared in the plane's door. The usual official welcoming party presented Mrs. Kennedy with a vivid bouquet of red roses. Even though the proceedings were already behind schedule, as most political events usually are, Jack Kennedy had to stop and shake a few hands. A radiant Jackie joined him in the throng of outstretched hands and cameras (above). Dallas' greeting, like the 76° temperature, was warm and refreshing.

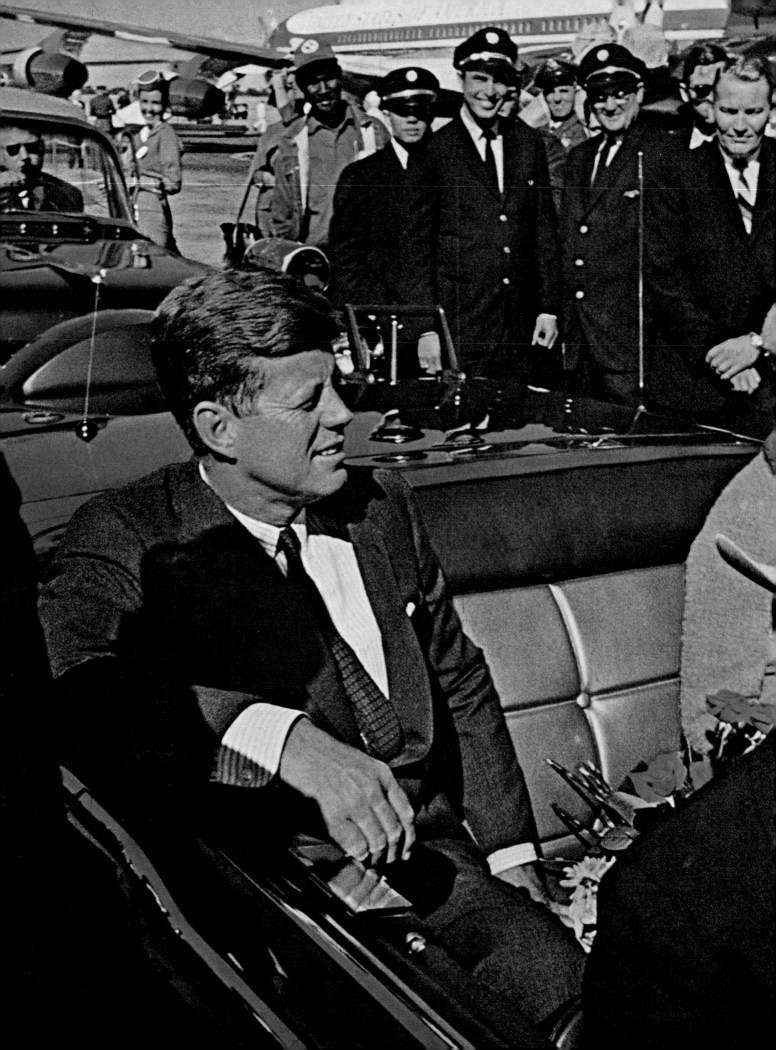

The motorcade

Bustling officials at last steered the President to his car so the motorcade could begin. It was to follow a circuitous eleven-mile route through downtown Dallas to the Trade Mart, where the President would speak. The big presidential Lincoln limousine had been flown from Washington for the occasion, and because of the pleasant weather, its plastic bubble top was removed and the bullet-proof side windows rolled down. President and Mrs. Kennedy settled in the back seat, with Governor and Mrs. Connally taking the jump seats just in front of them. At 11:50 A.M. the motorcade began to roll. The crowds were thick and exuberant. Kennedy frequently stood up and waved. Then, at a point where the crowds thinned out, the President settled back in his seat to chat with the Connallys.

Sniper's post

The motorcade route took the presidential car around a sharp left turn and down an incline toward a triple underpass. Looming over the turn is an old seven-story brick building, a warehouse called the Texas School Book Depository. From the windows of the upper floors (an infrequently visited area used for dead storage) there is an unobstructed view of the roadway below. Standing at a sixth-floor window (above) was the most intent spectator of the many thousands who watched the motorcade. He was tracking the limousine through the telescopic sight of a rifle. What he saw is re-created in the picture at right, photographed from the same spot through an identical sight. As the Lincoln reached the point indicated by the arrow in the picture above, Mrs. Connally turned smilingly to the President and said, "You can't say that Dallas isn't friendly to you today." Jack Kennedy's reply was cut off by the sharp, brutal sound of a gunshot.

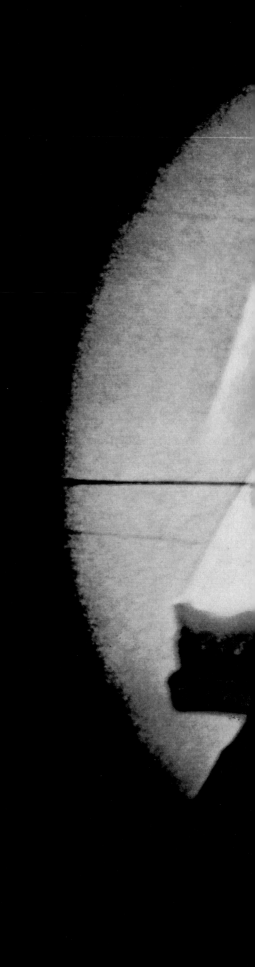

Three shots

These startling pictures, taken from an 8 mm. color film, show the brief, terrible moments that shook the world. At the crack of the shot, the President jerked sharply and clutched his neck. Governor Connally, sitting directly ahead of him, turned back toward the sound and was immediately tumbled into his wife's arms by a second shot. As Kennedy slumped forward a third shot was fired. The man visible beyond the limousine in the left-hand picture, holding his little boy's hand, said later that this third shot "seemed to just knock him down." One of the motorcycle-escort policemen said that the President's "head exploded in blood" at the impact of the bullet. In the right-hand picture, the driver slams on the brakes and the police escort pulls up. Jacqueline Kennedy, crying "Jack! Oh, no! No!" reaches for her stricken husband. The frightful sequence was over in less than six seconds.

Overleaf: A spectator standing at the curb took this close-up picture seconds after the bullets struck.

Even as the last shot was fired, Secret Service agents in the car behind the President's jumped out, brandishing automatic weapons. But there was no one to shoot at. In the photograph above, agent Clint Hill leaps toward the back of the limousine. Opposite, in stills from another film sequence documenting the tragedy, Mrs. Kennedy starts to climb across the back of the car (top) to assist Hill, who has just put one foot on the bumper. Governor and Mrs. Connally have fallen to the floor of the car. Beyond, a man in a red shirt (seen starting to react in the picture on this page) begins to run, panic-stricken. Opposite, below, Clint Hill is on the rear deck of the car and Jacqueline Kennedy moves back into the seat to aid her husband as the car races off. Three witnesses remain transfixed.

Flash from Dallas

Just as Secret Service men reacted instinctively, rushing to protect the presidential party, reporters reacted instinctively to get the news—sketchy as it was at first—to the world. United Press International's Merriman Smith, dean of the White House correspondents, describes on pages 32–33 his frantic rush to call the Dallas UPI bureau. Reproduced here is the result of Smith's first efforts—the actual Teletype copy that almost immediately clacked out of hundreds of UPI machines in newsrooms, radio and television stations, pressrooms, and business offices all over the world.

```
DETECTIVES WERE THERE AND THEY "ASKED HIM TO LOOK IN THERE (THE BRIEF-
CASE) FOR SOMETHING."
     THE CASE WAS OPENED AND AN ENVELOPE WAS FOUND CONTAINING 44 $100
BILLS, THE WITNESS SAID. THE STATE HAD SAID IT WOULD PRODUCE THAT
PIECE OF EVIDENCE BUT IT HAD  NOT  LISTED IT AS ONE "OF THE SEVEN
LINKS." THE DEFENSE HAS IMPLIED IT WILL TAKE THE LINE THAT CAROL'S
DEATH AFTER A SAVAGE BLUDGEONING AND STABBING IN HER HOME WAS THE
RESULT OF AN ATTEMPTED        MOREDA1234PCS



UPI A7N DA
          PRECEDE KENNEDY
     DALLAS, NOV. 22 (UPI)--THREE SHOTS WERE FIRED AT PRESIDENT KENNEDY'S
MOTORCADE TODAY IN DOWNTOWN DALLAS.
                          JT1234PCS..



UPI A8N HX
2ND ADD 2ND LEAD   THOMPSON MINNEAPOLIST
BUOS HO
UPHOLD
DA IT YRS  NX



UPI A8N AJ
DAY
     CORRECTE
BUOS UPHOLD--NX



UPI A8N DA
          URGENT
     1ST ADD SHOTS, DALLAS (A7N) XXX DOWNTOWN DALLAS.
     NO CASUALTIES WERE REPORTED.
     THE INCIDENT OCCURRED NEAR THE COUNTY SHERIFF'S OFFICE ON MAIN
STREET, JUST EAST OF AN UNDERPASS LEADING TOWARD THE TRADE MART WHERE
THE PRESIDENT WAS TO MA

                    FLASH


FLASH
     KENNEDY SERIOUSLY WOUNDED
                    PERHAPS SERIOUSLY
     PERHAPS FATALLY BY ASSASSINS BULLET
                    JT1239PCS
```

At 12:34 the Teletype was supplying copy on a Minneapolis murder trial.

The Dallas bureau, alerted by Smith over radiotelephone from the press car as it careered toward the hospital, sends out the first sparse news.

Minneapolis starts to add more details on the murder trial. The New York bureau, knowing that ace reporter Smith is covering the President's trip, tells all bureaus to "uphold"—get off the wire. "Dallas, it's yours."

Atlanta tries to interrupt, but is quickly squelched by the New York bureau.

The Dallas operator begins sending the rest of Smith's account from the press car.

At the hospital, Smith sees the President's limp body in the car and races to a telephone. At 12:39, nine minutes after the shooting, the grave news flashes over the wire.

```
UPI 9N
BULLETIN
   1ST LEAD SHOOTING
   DALLAS, NOV. 22 (UPI)--PRESIDENT KENNEDY AND GOV. JOHN B. CONNALLY
OF TEXAS WERE CUTDOWN BY AN ASSASSIN'S BULLETS AS THEY TOURED
DOWNTOWN DALLAS IN AN OPEN AUTOMOBILE TODAY.
                              MOREJT1241PCS



UPI A10N DA
         1ST ADD 1ST LEAD SHOOTING DALLAS (9N DALLAS XX TODAY.
   THE PRESIDENT, HIS LIMP BODY CRADLED IN THE ARMS OF HIS WIFE, WAS
RUSHED TO PARKLAND HOSPITAL.  THE GOVERNOR ALSO WAS TAKEN TO PARKLAND.
   CLINT HILL, A SECRET SERVICE AGENT ASSIGNED TO MRS. KENNEDY, SAID
"HE'S DEAD," AS THE PRESIDENT WAS LIFTED FROM THE REAR OF A WHITE HOUSE
TOURING CAR, THE FAMOUS "BUBBLETOP" FROM WASHINGTON.  HE WAS RUSHED
TO AN EMERGENCY ROOM IN THE HOSPITAL.
   OTHER WHITE HOUSE OFFICIALS WERE IN DOUBT AS THE CORRIDORS OF THE
HOSPITAL ERUPTED IN PANDEMONIUM.
   THE INCIDENT OCCURRED JUST EAST OF THE TRIPLE UNDERPASS FACING A
PARK IN DOWNTOWN DALLAS.
   REPORTERS ABOUT FIVE CAR LENGTHS BEHIND THE CHIEF EXECUTIVE
HEAR
MORE 144PES



UPI A11N DA
         2ND ADD 1ST LEAD SHOOTING (9N DALLAS) XXX DALLAS.
   REPORTERS ABOUT FIVE CAR LENGTHS BEHIND THE CHIEF EXECUTIVE
HEARD WHAT WOUNDED LIKE THREE BURST OF GUNFIRE.
   SECRET SERVICE AGENTS IN A FOLLOW-UP CAR QUICKLY UNLIMBERED THEIR
AUTOMATIC RIFLES.
   THE BUBBLE TOP OF THE PRESIDENT'S CAR WAS DOWN.
   THEY DREW THEIR PISTOLS, BUT THE DAMAGE WAS DONE.
   THE PRESIDENT WAS SLUMPED OVER IN THE BACKSEAT OF THE CAR FACE
DOWN.  CONNALLY LAY ON THE FLOOR OF THE REAR SEAT.
   IT WAS IMPOSSIBLE TO TELL AT
MORE 145PES



UPI A12N DA

   IT WAS IMPOSSIBLE TO TELL AT ONCE WHERE KENNEDY WAS HIT, BUT BULLET
WOUNDS IN CONNALLY'S CHEST WERE PLAINLY VISIBLE, INDICATING THE GUNFIRE
MIGHT POSSIBLY HAVE COME FROM AN AUTOMATIC WEAPON.
   THERE WERE THREE LOUD BURSTS.
   DALLAS MOTORCYCLE OFFICERS ESCORTING THE PRESIDENT QUICKLY LEAPED
FROM THEIR BIKES AND RACED UP A GRASSY HILL.

   MORE 146PES



UPIA13N DA
```

Now reporter Smith is dictating a story ready for printing.

Smith rolls on, swiftly and fluently, adding fresh details as "pandemonium" breaks out in the corridor outside his telephone niche.

Searching his mind for impressions of the shooting, Smith adds all he can remember to the story. The shaken wire operator stumbles in the second line.

As yet nothing is known of the sniper, what kind of weapon he used, or where the shots came from.

A moment after the scene on pages 20 and 21, the presidential limousine roars away from the scene of the shooting, with Secret Service agent Hill clinging to the back of the car (above), shielding the occupants. At left is the tableau in its wake: a man and woman lie on the ground, covering their children to protect them from the mysterious shots (these are the witnesses visible beyond the car in the picture on page 16), while a cameraman tries to record the fleeing auto. Opposite: The car (with its convertible top up now) stands before the emergency entrance of Parkland Hospital just after the President and Governor Connally were carried inside.

To the hospital

Alerted by the police, a surgical team stood by in Emergency Room One of Parkland Memorial Hospital. Suddenly two Secret Service men burst into the room. One of them, his face contorted with anguish, was waving a sub-machine gun. Staff members dived for cover. A man in a business suit dashed in; the agent slammed him against the wall with one punch. Dazed, the man pulled out F.B.I. credentials and gasped, "I've got to call J. Edgar Hoover." A moment later the President and Governor Connally were carried into the hospital. A bullet was found to have penetrated Connally's chest and wrist and lodged in his thigh. The wound was serious, but not fatal. In Emergency Room One, doctors worked feverishly over the President. Jackie Kennedy stood quietly by, looking "brave—but fear was in her eyes." She called for a priest. An oxygen tube was inserted in the President's throat, and he was given transfusions of whole blood. In desperation, a doctor tried to stimulate his heart with chest massage. The doctor monitoring an electrocardiograph reported no heartbeat: "It's too late," he said quietly. A sheet was pulled over the body, and a priest arrived and administered the last rites. The hospital's chief surgeon said later, "I am absolutely sure he never knew what hit him." At 1:33 P.M. a press aide announced that the President of the United States was dead.

"My God, what are we coming to?"

So exclaimed House Speaker John McCormack when he heard the news in Washington. As the stunning word flashed around the globe, people great and small simply stopped and stared in disbelief. First came tears, then halting words. "Your thoughts just don't work at a time like this," said a Negro doorman in Atlanta. A college student felt "as if the end of the world had come along, and you're not prepared for it." The Stars and Stripes fluttered to half-staff across the nation and at America's outposts across the world. In the Senate the chaplain said, "We gaze at a vacant place against the sky, as the President of the Republic goes down like a giant cedar."

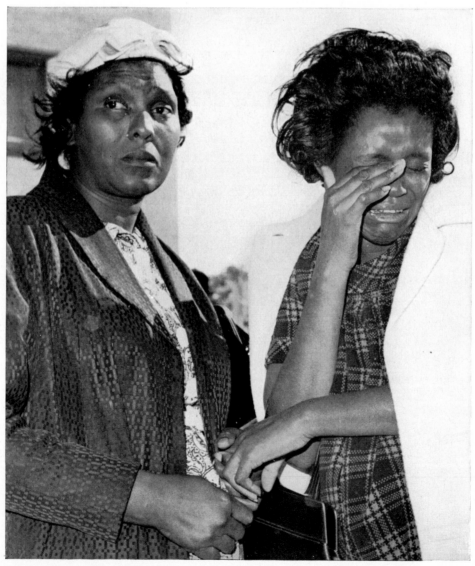

Two women grieve
outside the hospital in Dallas.

At his Virginia home,
Attorney General Robert Kennedy
is comforted by his children.

Texas Senator Ralph Yarborough, a witness to the assassination, tries to talk to reporters.
Right: The White House, minutes after the President's death.

The manhunt begins

Within minutes of the assassination, police surrounded the Texas School Book Depository building, from where the shots seemed to have come. A photographer had glimpsed a rifle being quickly withdrawn into a sixth-floor window (arrow).

Swarming through the book warehouse, police soon found the sniper's post on the sixth floor. The killer had stacked up cartons so that he could not be seen from the next building. Three cartons served as a rest for his rifle.

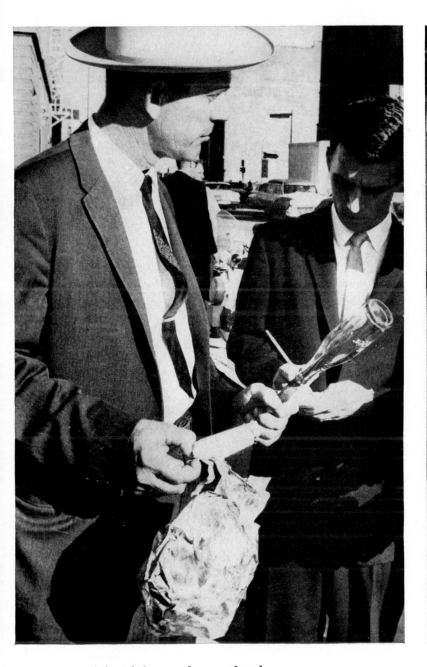

A lunch bag and a pop bottle, held here by a Dallas police technician, and three spent shell casings were found by the sixth-floor window. The sniper had dined on fried chicken and pop while waiting patiently to shoot the President.

A Dallas detective holds the rifle thought to be the murder weapon. It was found on the fifth floor of the warehouse, carelessly (or hurriedly) hidden behind book cartons. The gun was rushed to the crime lab at police headquarters for tests.

Police cars draw up in front of the Dallas movie theatre (above) where Lee Harvey Oswald is seized. At right, Oswald shakes a fist at reporters inside police headquarters: "I haven't shot anybody!" he yelled.

Dallas patrolman J. D. Tippit, who was murdered within forty-five minutes of the President's assassination.

A suspect is captured

Shortly after the assassination, the police radio broadcast a description of an employee missing from the schoolbook warehouse. At 1:15—fifteen minutes after the President died—patrolman J. D. Tippit spotted a man answering the description some two miles from the assassination scene. Tippit stepped from his squad car to question him and was shot three times and killed instantly. Witnesses saw the gunman run through a vacant lot, ejecting shells from a pistol. Minutes later a shoe-store manager saw a man jump into the store's doorway as a police car sped by, then hurry down the street and into a movie theatre. Suspicious, the manager spoke to the theatre cashier, who called police. At 1:45, as detectives searched the theatre, a man jumped up, drew a .38-caliber pistol, and shouted, "This is it!" His gun misfired, and he was subdued after a scuffle and taken to police headquarters. Reporters were told that one Lee Harvey Oswald was a "hot suspect" in the murders of patrolman J. D. Tippit and President John F. Kennedy.

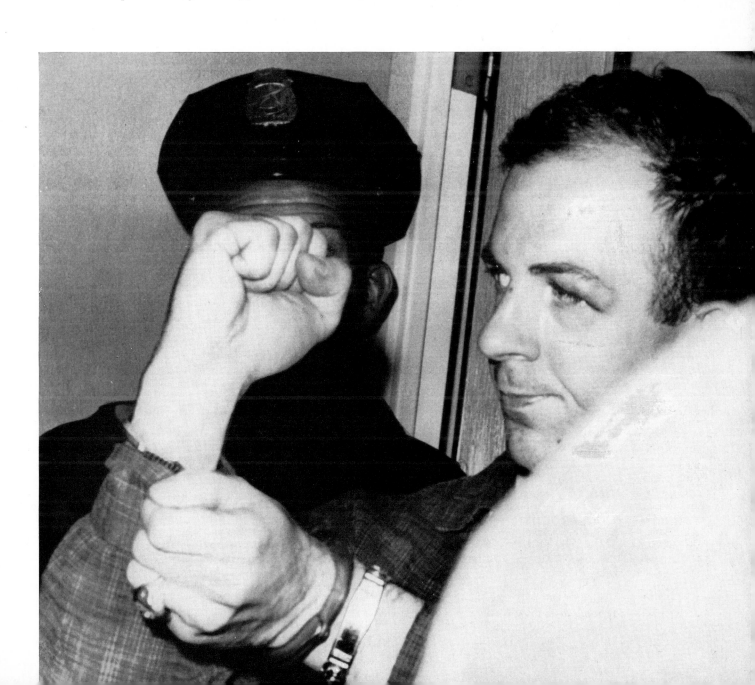

Eyewitness account

*UPI's brilliant reporter, Merriman Smith,
was an eyewitness to the momentous events.
Here is his story, dispatched the next day.*

By Merriman Smith
UPI White House Reporter

Washington, Nov. 23 (UPI) — It was a balmy, sunny noon as we motored through downtown Dallas behind President Kennedy. The procession cleared the center of the business district and turned into a handsome highway that wound through what appeared to be a park.

I was riding in the so-called White House press "pool" car, a telephone company vehicle equipped with a mobile radio-telephone. I was in the front seat between a driver from the telephone company and Malcolm Kilduff, acting White House press secretary for the President's Texas tour. Three other pool reporters were wedged in the back seat.

Suddenly we heard three loud, almost painfully loud cracks. The first sounded as if it might have been a large firecracker. But the second and third blasts were unmistakable. Gunfire.

The President's car, possibly as much as 150 or 200 yards ahead, seemed to falter briefly. We saw a flurry of activity in the Secret Service follow-up car behind the Chief Executive's bubble-top limousine.

Next in line was the car bearing Vice President Lyndon B. Johnson. Behind that, another follow-up car bearing agents assigned to the Vice President's protection. We were behind that car.

Our car stood still for probably only a few seconds, but it seemed like a lifetime. One sees history explode before one's eyes and for even the most trained observer, there is a limit to what one can comprehend.

I looked ahead at the President's car but could not see him or his companion, Gov. John B. Connally of Texas. Both men had been riding on the right side of the bubble-top limousine from Washington. I thought I saw a flash of pink which would have been Mrs. Jacqueline Kennedy.

Everybody in our car began shouting at the driver to pull up closer to the President's car. But at this moment, we saw the big bubble-top and a motorcycle escort roar away at high speed.

We screamed at our driver, "Get going, get going." We careened around the Johnson car and its escort and set out down the highway, barely able to keep in sight of the President's car and the accompanying Secret Service follow-up car.

They vanished around a curve. When we cleared the same curve we could see where we were heading—Parkland Hospital, a large brick structure to the left of the arterial highway. We skidded around a sharp left turn and spilled out of the pool car as it entered the hospital driveway.

I ran to the side of the bubble-top.

The President was face down on the back seat. Mrs. Kennedy made a cradle of her arms around the President's head and bent over him as if she were whispering to him.

Gov. Connally was on his back on the floor of the car, his head and shoulders resting in the arms of his wife, Nellie, who kept shaking her head and shaking with dry sobs. Blood oozed from the front of the Governor's suit. I could not see the President's wound. But I could see blood spattered around the interior of the rear seat and a dark stain spreading down the right side of the President's dark gray suit.

From the telephone car, I had radioed the Dallas bureau of UPI that three shots had been fired at the Kennedy motorcade. Seeing the bloody scene in the rear of the car at the hospital entrance, I knew I had to get to a telephone immediately.

Clint Hill, the Secret Service agent in charge of the detail assigned to Mrs. Kennedy, was leaning over into the rear of the car.

"How badly was he hit, Clint?" I asked.

"He's dead," Hill replied curtly.

I have no further clear memory of the scene in the driveway. I recall a babble of anxious voices, tense voices—"Where in hell are the stretchers. . . . Get a doctor out here . . . He's on the way . . . Come on, easy there." And from somewhere, nervous sobbing.

I raced down a short stretch of sidewalk into a hospital corridor. The first thing I spotted was a small clerical office, more of a booth than an office. Inside, a bespectacled man stood shuffling what appeared to be hospital forms. At a wicket much like a bank teller's cage, I spotted a telephone on the shelf.

"How do you get outside?" I gasped. "The President has been hurt and this is an emergency call."

"Dial nine," he said, shoving the phone toward me.

It took two tries before I successfully dialed the Dallas UPI number. Quickly I dictated a bulletin saying the President had been seriously, perhaps fatally, injured by an assassin's bullets while driving through the streets of Dallas.

Litters bearing the President and the Governor rolled by me as I dictated, but my back was to the hallway and I didn't see them until they were at the entrance of the emergency room about 75 or 100 feet away.

I knew they had passed, however, from the horrified expression that suddenly spread over the face of the man behind the wicket.

As I stood in the drab buff hallway leading into the emergency ward trying to reconstruct the shooting for the UPI man on the other end of the telephone and still keep track of what was happening outside the door of the emergency room, I watched a swift and confused panorama sweep before me.

Kilduff of the White House press staff raced up and down the hall. Police captains barked at each other, "Clear this area." Two priests hurried in behind a Secret Service agent, their narrow purple stoles rolled up tightly in their hands. A police lieutenant ran down the hall with a large carton of blood for transfusions. A doctor came in and said he was responding to a call for "all neurosurgeons."

The priests came out and said the President had received the last sacrament of the Roman Catholic Church. They said he was still alive, but not conscious. Members of the Kennedy staff began arriving. They had been behind us in the motorcade, but hopelessly bogged for a time in confused traffic.

Telephones were at a premium in the hospital and I clung to mine for dear life. I was afraid to stray from the wicket lest I lose contact with the outside world.

My decision was made for me, however, when Kilduff and Wayne Hawks of the White House staff ran by me, shouting that Kilduff would make a statement shortly in the so-called nurses' room a floor above and at the far end of the hospital.

I threw down the phone and sped after them. We reached the door of the conference room and there were loud cries of "Quiet!" Fighting to keep his emotions under control, Kilduff said, "President John Fitzgerald Kennedy died at approximately one o'clock."

I raced into a nearby office. The telephone switchboard at the hospital was hopelessly jammed.

Frustrated by the inability to get through the hospital switchboard, I appealed to a nurse. She led me through a maze of corridors and back stairways to another floor and a lone pay booth. I got the Dallas office.

[Afterward] I ran back through the hospital to the conference room. There Jiggs Fauver of the White House transportation staff grabbed me and said Kilduff wanted a pool of three men immediately to fly back to Washington on Air Force One, the presidential aircraft.

"He wants you downstairs, and he wants you right now," Fauver said.

Down the stairs I ran and into the driveway, only to discover Kilduff had just pulled out in our telephone car.

Charles Roberts of *Newsweek* magazine, Sid Davis of Westinghouse Broadcasting and I implored a police officer to take us to the airport in his squad car.

As we piled out of the car on the edge of the runway about 200 yards from the presidential aircraft, Kilduff spotted us and motioned for us to hurry. We trotted to him and he said the plane could take two pool men to Washington; that Johnson was soon to take the oath of office aboard the plane and would take off immediately thereafter.

I saw a bank of telephone booths beside the runway and asked if I had time to advise my news service. He said, "But for God's sake, hurry."

Then began another telephone nightmare. The Dallas office rang busy. I tried calling Washington. All circuits were busy. Then I called the New York bureau of UPI and told them about the impending installation of a new President aboard the airplane.

Kilduff came out of the plane and motioned wildly toward my booth. I slammed down the phone and jogged across the runway. A detective stopped me and said, "You dropped your pocket comb."

Aboard Air Force One on which I had made so many trips as a press association reporter covering President Kennedy, all of the shades of the larger main cabin were drawn and the interior was hot and dimly lighted.

Kilduff propelled us to the President's suite two-thirds of the way back in the plane. The room is used normally as a combination conference and sitting room and could accommodate eight to ten people seated.

I wedged inside the door and began counting. There were 27 people in this compartment. Johnson stood in the center with his wife, Lady Bird. U.S. District Judge Sarah T. Hughes, 67, a kindly faced woman, stood with a small black Bible in her hands, waiting to give the oath.

The compartment became hotter and hotter. Johnson was worried that some of the Kennedy staff might not be able to get inside. He urged people to press forward, but a Signal Corps photographer, Capt. Cecil Stoughton, standing in the corner on a chair, said if Johnson moved any closer, it would be virtually impossible to make a truly historic photograph.

It developed that Johnson was waiting for Mrs. Kennedy, who was composing herself in a small bedroom in the rear of the plane. She appeared alone, dressed in the same pink wool suit she had worn in the morning when she appeared so happy shaking hands with airport crowds at the side of her husband.

She was white-faced but dry-eyed. Friendly hands stretched toward her as she stumbled slightly. Johnson took both of her hands in his and motioned her to his left side. Lady Bird stood on his right, a fixed half-smile showing the tension.

Johnson nodded to Judge Hughes, an old friend of his family and a Kennedy appointee.

"Hold up your right hand and repeat after me," the woman jurist said to Johnson.

Outside a jet could be heard droning into a landing.

Judge Hughes held out the Bible and Johnson covered it with his large left hand. His right arm went slowly into the air and the jurist began to intone the Constitutional oath, "I do solemnly swear I will faithfully execute the office of President of the United States . . ."

The brief ceremony ended when Johnson in a deep, firm voice, repeated after the judge, ". . . so help me God."

Johnson turned first to his wife, hugged her about the shoulders and kissed her on the cheek. Then he turned to Kennedy's widow, put his left arm around her and kissed her cheek.

As others in the group—some Texas Democratic House members, members of the Johnson and Kennedy staffs—moved toward the new President, he seemed to back away from any expression of felicitation.

The two-minute ceremony concluded at 3:38 P.M. EST and seconds later, the President said firmly, "Now, let's get airborne."

Col. James Swindal, pilot of the plane, a big gleaming silver and blue fan-jet, cut on the starboard engines immediately. Several persons, including Sid Davis of Westinghouse, left the plane at that time. The White House had room for only two pool reporters on the return flight and these posts were filled by Roberts and me, although at the moment we could find no empty seats.

At 3:47 P.M. EST, the wheels of Air Force One cleared the runway. Swindal roared the big ship up to an unusually high cruising altitude of 41,000 feet where at 625 miles an hour, ground speed, the jet hurtled toward Andrews Air Force Base.

When the President's plane reached operating altitude, Mrs. Kennedy left her bedchamber and walked to the rear compartment of the plane. This was the so-called family living room, a private area where she and Kennedy, family and friends had spent many happy airborne hours chatting and dining together.

Kennedy's casket had been placed in this compartment, carried aboard by a group of Secret Service agents.

Mrs. Kennedy went into the rear lounge and took a chair beside the coffin. There she remained throughout the flight. Her vigil was shared at times by four staff members close to the slain chief executive—David Powers, his buddy and personal assistant; Kenneth P. O'Donnell, appointments secretary and key political adviser; Lawrence O'Brien, chief Kennedy liaison man with Congress, and Brig. Gen. Godfrey McHugh, Kennedy's Air Force aide.

Kennedy's military aide, Maj. Gen. Chester V. Clifton, was busy most of the trip in the forward areas of the plane, sending messages and making arrangements for arrival ceremonies and movement of the body to Bethesda Naval Hospital.

As the flight progressed, Johnson walked back into the main compartment. My portable typewriter was lost somewhere around the hospital and I was writing on an over-sized electric typewriter which Kennedy's personal secretary, Mrs. Evelyn Lincoln, had used to type his speech texts.

Johnson came up to the table where Roberts and I were trying to record the history we had just witnessed.

"I'm going to make a short statement in a few minutes and give you copies of it," he said. "Then when I get on the ground, I'll do it over again."

It was the first public utterance of the new Chief Executive, brief and moving.

When the plane was about 45 minutes from Washington, the new President got on a special radio-telephone and placed a call to Mrs. Rose Kennedy, the late President's mother.

"I wish to God there was something I could do," he told her, "I just wanted you to know that."

Then Mrs. Johnson wanted to talk to the elder Mrs. Kennedy.

"We feel like the heart has been cut out of us," Mrs. Johnson said. She broke down for a moment and began to sob. Recovering in a few seconds, she added, "Our love and our prayers are with you."

Thirty minutes out of Washington, Johnson put in a call for Nellie Connally, wife of the seriously wounded Texas Governor.

The new President said to the Governor's wife:

"We are praying for you, darling, and I know that everything is going to be all right, isn't it? Give him a hug and a kiss for me."

It was dark when Air Force One began to skim over the lights of the Washington area, lining up for a landing at Andrews Air Force Base. The plane touched down at 5:59 P.M. EST.

The 36th President

Standing in the crowded cabin of the President's plane, between his wife and Mrs. Kennedy, Lyndon Johnson takes the oath of office:

"I do solemnly swear that I will faithfully execute the office of President of the United States, and will to the best of my ability, preserve, protect, and defend the Constitution of the United States. So help me God."
  —*Lyndon Baines Johnson*
  2:38 P.M. CST
  November 22, 1963

Arrival in Washington

Shortly after 6 P.M. Eastern standard time, Air Force One, its engines cut, rolled quietly and eerily into a circle of light at Andrews Air Force base near Washington. A yellow lift truck edged up to the open door to receive a bronze casket bearing the body of John Kennedy. The casket was placed in an ambulance, and Jacqueline Kennedy, proud and straight, joined her husband. Only after the ambulance was gone did the new President step to center stage. Before microphones and television cameras, with his wife at his side, Lyndon Johnson began to speak to a hushed and grieving nation.

A new President speaks to the nation

At Andrews Air Force Base,
with his wife at his side,
President Johnson reads his first
public statement: "This is a sad time
for all people. We have suffered a
loss that cannot be weighed. For me
it is a deep personal tragedy.
I know the world shares the sorrow
that Mrs. Kennedy and her
family bear. I will do my best.
That is all I can do.
I ask for your help—and God's."

Left: The President's body is
borne in an ambulance to
the White House to lie in repose.
Below: The flag-draped coffin
is carried into the White House.
Right: Still close to her husband,
a sleepless Jacqueline Kennedy
walks behind the coffin.

Home to the White House

The long day was drawing to a close. From Dallas came word that Lee H. Oswald had been arraigned for the murder of Patrolman Tippit. Asked about the assassination, Homicide Captain Will Fitz replied, "We have some more work to do on that case." In Washington, President Johnson met with Administration and congressional leaders and, at 9:24 left for his home. After midnight came further word from Dallas: Oswald was now charged with the assassination. The day's final act took place just before dawn. An ambulance drove slowly up the White House driveway behind a crisp Marine honor guard. John Fitzgerald Kennedy had come home.

SATURDAY

23

NOV. 1963

Saturday was a day out of time, a day in which crowds stood mutely in the cold drizzle, watching the White House, waiting for something to happen that did not happen. Tens of millions of Americans sat in front of their television sets listening to reporters who had nothing to report. The violence and shock of the previous day had been transmuted into the clean, precise formality of a catafalque in the East Room of the White House. John Fitzgerald Kennedy lay in state.

The few real events of Saturday seemed rather unreal, engulfed as they were in a more tangible shroud of sorrow. While the nation began to mourn its dead President, the new President got on with the business of the republic, meeting with his Secretary of State, his Secretary of Defense, with former Presidents Eisenhower and Truman, with congressional leaders. The world was told about Lyndon Johnson and assured that everything would be all right. Lee Harvey Oswald was taken from his cell on the fourth floor of Dallas Police Headquarters to the Homicide Bureau on the third floor, where his interrogation was resumed.

But the reality of the day was to be seen in the monotonous, gray procession of dignitaries filing into the White House to pay their respects, in the frozen figure of Sir Alec Douglas-Home kneeling in prayer at a requiem mass in Westminster Cathedral, in the faces of Frenchmen, halted for a moment that prolonged itself hypnotically into hours, in front of a television set in a Paris store window. Englishmen had walked miles to stand in the rain, weeping, in front of London's American Embassy. Berliners rose in the dark, early-morning hours to walk with torches through the streets of the city. In Berne, Switzerland, torches flamed above the heads of weeping marchers, points of light flickering endlessly into space. And in Dallas wreaths were placed on the spot where John Kennedy had been murdered. America was in a state of suspension, and for a time the world seemed to stand silently still.

In the midst of the unrelenting grief was the ineluctable dismay that for all that might be said on that day, for all that might be done in homage, it was then, irrevocably, too little and too late.

Saturday vigil

The harsh ugliness of Friday had, by Saturday morning, been elevated to a somber majesty in the still, grave surroundings of the White House. A military honor guard and two priests kept vigil in the East Room. The Kennedy family, after a private mass at the closed coffin, had left the room at 10:30. President Kennedy's body lay in a flag-draped coffin. The hangings in the East Room, at Mrs. Kennedy's request, were similar to those used nearly one hundred years before when Lincoln had lain there.

Flat 3, 40 Trumlands Road, St. Marychurch, Torquay, Devon.
Tel.: Torquay 87766.

23 Nov. 1963

Miss Rose Russell.

Oh, my dear Rose,

What a terrible thing has happened to us all! To you there, to us here, to all everywhere. Peace who was becoming bright-eyed now sits in the shadow of death: her handsome champion has been killed as he walked by her very side. Her gallant boy is dead.

What a cruel, foul, and most unnatural murder!

We mourn here with you poor, sad American people.

Sean

The words of the 79-year-old Irish poet Sean O'Casey, in a letter to a friend in New York (above), were typical of the response from abroad. "What a terrible thing has happened to us all!" he said. At right, Britain's Prime Minister, Sir Alec Douglas-Home, kneels in prayer at Westminster Cathedral; Konrad Adenauer, above opposite, and Nikita Khrushchev, below opposite, signed books in Bonn and Moscow. "It was with deep personal grief," Mr. Khrushchev wrote to Mrs. Kennedy, "that I learned about the tragic death of your husband. . . ."

World reaction

Statesmen did more than mourn the loss of another statesman. Premier Khrushchev lamented the blow the President's death dealt Soviet-American relations; Mrs. Khrushchev wept. And for a moment at least, political and personal feelings seemed to fuse. "Everything in one cried out in protest," Sir Alec Douglas-Home said. "This young, gay and brave statesman, killed in the full vigor of his manhood, when he bore on his shoulders all the cares and hopes of the world. . . ."

Berlin: a new square

Berlin: torches in the street

Tokyo: Buddhist prayers

Tokyo: silence in a department store

Paris: like other homes

The world's grief

In almost every country there was mourning. People wept, prayed, stood silent in the streets, or lit torches to parade sadly through the night. From such spontaneous demonstrations, Americans learned how many people of other lands considered Kennedy *their* President. The loss they felt was the loss of one who seemed a personal friend as well as a world leader.

Nairobi: a proclamation of pain

Paris: a radio on the street

Seoul: sidewalk bulletins

London: flags at half-staff

Moscow: sober readers
Overleaf: torchlight procession in Berne, Switzerland

Early on Saturday morning Lyndon Johnson
rode in a rain-splattered car to his first
full day of work as President. Johnson's succession,
his immediate assumption of the burdens
of office even before the first dignitaries had
paid their respects to the dead President,
affirmed the order and stability of the republic,
whose first magistrates have succeeded one
another now in an unbroken continuity since
1789. This succession is a record among
democracies, unmatched anywhere, but it was
only in such reflections that anyone might
take comfort this morning. The new President's
first act was a proclamation that set Monday
as a national day of mourning.

THE WHITE HOUSE

By the President of the United States of America

A Proclamation

To the People of the United States:

John Fitzgerald Kennedy, 35th President of the United States, has been taken from us by an act which outrages decent men everywhere.

He upheld the faith of our Fathers, which is freedom for all men. He broadened the frontiers of that faith, and backed it with the energy and the courage which are the mark of the Nation he led.

A man of wisdom, strength and peace, he molded and moved the power of our Nation in the service of a world of growing liberty and order. All who love freedom will mourn his death.

As he did not shrink from his responsibilities, but welcomed them, so he would not have us shrink from carrying on his work beyond this hour of national tragedy.

He said it himself: "The energy, the faith, the devotion which we bring to this endeavor will light our country and all who serve it—and the glow from that fire can truly light the world."

Now, therefore, I, Lyndon B. Johnson, President of the United States of America, do appoint Monday next, November 25, the day of the funeral service of President Kennedy, to be a day of national mourning throughout the United States. I earnestly recommend the people to assemble on that day in their respective places of divine worship, there to bow down in submission to the will of Almighty God, and to pay their homage of love and reverence to the memory of a great and good man. I invite the people of the world who share our grief to join us in this day of mourning and rededication.

IN WITNESS WHEREOF, I have hereunto set my hand and caused the Seal of the United States of America to be affixed.

DONE at the City of Washington this twenty-third day of November in the year of our Lord nineteen hundred and sixty-three, and of the Independence of the United States of America the one hundredth and eighty-eighth.

LYNDON B. JOHNSON

The line of succession

The new regime—so the world was told—would continue the policies and the vigorous leadership of the Kennedy Administration. And the world hoped it was true, hoped there would be continuity of spirit as well as policy. But, as dreary hour followed dreary hour on Saturday, reports filtered back to Washington from other nations: Britain had doubts; Germany was uncertain; Argentina was concerned; France was fearful. Americans, still held in dumb attentiveness at their television sets, watched the parade of the new order, and recalled that Johnson had had a heart attack in 1955. Next in the line of succession was John McCormack, a man seventy-one years of age, then Carl Hayden, eighty-six years old. Watching McCormack and Hayden arrive at the White House, Americans could hardly help but recall John Kennedy's youth and vigor.

Left: President Johnson arrives at the East Room of the White House at 11 A.M., accompanied by his wife and by Speaker of the House John McCormack, who is first in line to succeed Johnson to the office of President.

Carl Hayden, second in the new line of succession, is helped up the steps of the White House Saturday morning to view Kennedy's coffin.

Even before paying respects to Mr. Kennedy, Johnson conferred with his Cabinet. He spoke with Secretary of State Dean Rusk at 9:20 A.M.

After visiting the catafalque Johnson returned to the Executive Office Building to resume his duties, and to speak with General Eisenhower.

The public manner

When the moment came for statesmen to view the catafalque, nearly every man, as he placed his foot on the top step at the entrance to the White House, had to catch at himself for an instant to regain his public manner. The Russian Ambassador, Anatoly Dobrynin (left) maintained his poise with a merely grim expression. Former President Truman (right) covered his sadness with anxiousness. Henry Cabot Lodge (far right) found it necessary to bite his lip. Chief Justice Earl Warren and his wife had managed to enter the White House without loss of composure, but Mrs. Warren could not restrain her tears as they left (below). Americans who were watching the dignitaries were told that the eight-year-old daughter of Nigeria's Minister of State, K. O. Mbadiwe, had recited to her father, from memory, Kennedy's entire inaugural address. As she spoke, he cried.

Departure from
the White House

It was odd that, of all personal objects, the one that most clearly recalled the youngest President America ever elected was a rocking chair. The unceremonious removal of the rocker signified the departure of John Kennedy, and the beginning of a new administration in Washington. It was taken out through a side door of the White House executive offices, unseen by those who kept watch (above) in Lafayette Square. On the day after the funeral Lyndon Johnson moved into the President's office. With him, from his home in Spring Valley, he brought a new rocking chair.

Town in torment

While visitors filed past John Kennedy's coffin in Washington, as Lyndon Johnson assumed the tasks of the Presidency, UPI correspondent H. D. Quigg returned to the place of the assassination in Dallas to capture the mood of that stricken city.

By H. D. Quigg

Dallas (UPI) — The flowers wilt now on the cool grass. Beside the gray pavement where the shots echoed, the wreaths lie on the green. And the ache lingers in the hearts of Dallas. The noise of bullets that entered bone and flesh is yesterday's. No longer heard, and yet, you think as you watch the throngs go by and linger at the spot and drop their wreaths of mourning and just look and look and no noise comes—you think: maybe they hear the way the sad poet did when he said, ". . . as I stand by the roadside, or on the pavement gray, I hear it in the deep heart's core."

For the heart of Dallas is in the little cards attached to the wreaths dropped on patches of green grass on either side of the gray strip. If Walt Whitman could write, of the dead Lincoln, "When lilacs last in the dooryard bloomed," so Dallas writes—not with a poet's pretense. But with words pulled out hard and felt so deeply and then given the bloom of flowers to lay at the dooryard of death. Here, for one, some red and white carnations, with a bit of greenery mixed, and the card pinned on with its printed line of standard stuff for wreaths: "Deepest sympathy." But on the white space underneath in blue ink in a feminine hand:

> "We love You—
> Please Forgive us—
> The Ted Wilson Family"

"God forgive us all," another says, and stops there. And another: "In memory of our President, whom we loved dearly."

A sprig with a white ribbon tied around it has a note written with red crayon: "I'm sorry Caroline and John John. Forgive us. A 9-year old Dallas girl."

Dallas never felt so alone. Joe M. Dealey, grandson of the community builder whose great bronze statue stands in the park where John F. Kennedy was shot through the brain, expressed the first-felt pang to a reporter: "We are a tormented town."

And the proud and sovereign state of Texas feels, too, that the old song that told you the eyes of Texas are upon you, all the livelong day, might have had some updating. In a memorial service before the capitol in Austin, a state judge said: ". . . the eyes of the world are upon us—and they will be looking with a critical stare."

It is an old man speaking. They call him "Mr. Dallas." His name is R. L. Thornton but he's known everywhere as Mayor Thornton—no man has ever matched his record of eight consecutive years in the office, ending in 1961. He has flowing white hair, pepper-and-salt eyebrows, and a lean and leathery look.

He points a knobby finger at you: "The President was on the streets of Dallas in a parade in which the people of Dallas were his hosts. This thing just numbed them.

"I'm eighty-four years old, and I've never had anything hit me so in my life. All I could do was pray. There was more prayer fell from the lips of the people of Dallas than anything that's ever hit it in its history. A fellow told me he prayed for twenty minutes. When the word went out, Dallas became an instant city of prayer.

"There's been very little business going on. [He ought to know; he's the founder and board chairman of the Mercantile National Bank.] People are just numb. They've got to get back on the track.

"I'm an old-timer here. Been here sixty years now. Come here from a farm in Ellis County. I'm saying to the people of Dallas: The only thing to do is pray—then roll up your sleeves. We'll be back at work Monday. We'll be lined up and at it in just a day or so. We'll go ahead and build Dallas as we have in the past."

The outpouring of prayer and church attendance was part of the burden of agonizing self-inspection. Four score and eighteen years ago, Abraham Lincoln lay in his coffin, and the Dallas *Herald* said then: "God Almighty ordered this event or it could never have taken place."

Three days after John F. Kennedy died, and one day after his alleged assassin died, the Dallas *Times Herald* said: "Even as we are staggered by one violent discharge of hate following another, the citizens of Dallas are surely engaging in the greatest spiritual self-examination any American community has undergone in this century. Dallas churches held massive, prayerful, sober crowds Sunday. . . . This was a pilgrimage, an act of civic penance compelled by an inexpressible feeling that all of us have contributed something to the atmosphere which has caused or allowed these acts to take place here. But in church or out, Dallas is a city undergoing the dark night of the soul, a city appealing to a Higher Power. . . ."

And indeed, on that Sunday, the grief was embodied in standing room only at more than six hundred churches in all services—including the largest Presbyterian, Methodist, and Baptist churches in the world, the second largest synagogue.

"There were more than 500,000 worshippers in all services," says Joe Dealey, president of the Dallas *Morning News*. The town's metropolitan area population as of 1962 was 1,152,215. It's a strong and proud city, ridden at first by some doubt and fear—and sudden anger, even of neighbor against neighbor. Now it's snapping back. But you know if you're here that Big D has been shaken—as if someone scruffed it, like a dog, and gave it a humiliating shake.

In the world's largest Methodist church, William H. Dickinson, Jr., wartime chaplain of the combat-famed 36th Division, spoke of the fine plans for the President's visit, of the dignified and sincere expression of honor and affection accorded him before "our world crumbled around us."

It was ironic, he said, that President Kennedy and Governor John Connally should be attacked by an extreme leftist whereas on October 24 Dallas made headlines when "extremists from the far right" held a demonstration in which U.N. Ambassador Adlai E. Stevenson was spat upon and struck by a picket's placard.

"Hate knows no political loyalty and is as dead and as vicious in the heart and mind of liberals and those to the far left as those to the far right alike . . ." he said.

Dallas, Texas, has class, confidence, culture, bustle, fashion, emergent sophistication, some swagger—and still a smattering of ten-gallon hats. But the wave of the present is on it—aerospace and electronics industries, mighty skyscrapers that soar with the aspiringest anywhere—and the majority of its males go hatless in the mode of J. F. K. It has a United States attorney who is named—and for real—Barefoot Sanders. Its citizens are friendly to a fault—it comes naturally—to strangers. It goes for football but not for big professional prize fights.

It is a city of conservative political thought, of go-go civic pride, of outspoken argument. Dallas County went for Truman in 1948—and he was the last Democratic presidential candidate to carry it. The mayor, Earle Cabell, (he was under police guard because his own life was threatened after Kennedy's assassination) called upon his people in the wake of the tragedy:

"Enter into controversy without hatred, disagreement without disparagement."

J. Erik Jonsson, head of the supragovernmental citizens council and the man who was waiting to host a luncheon at which President Kennedy was due just five minutes after the fatal shots were fired, says of charges of right-wing hate elements here:

"We've got a few spectaculars here who make the news—draw attention. Dallas is a conservative community. Both Republican and Democratic parties have strong conservative elements. Hate? This is an emotional reaction. If you look at any of our other cities dispassionately, we have less hate here than in most other communities. As for Oswald, this man wasn't a Dallasite. He had been here only a couple of months."

Joe Dealey says Lee Harvey Oswald was a "floater," who got his job here two or three days after the President's original announcement that he intended to visit Dallas.

He adds: "We have no hotbed of rightism here. We do have some extremely articulate exponents of it."

"We wanted to remain reasonably silent until the President was buried," said Erik Jonsson, "and then do something that reflects real sorrow for Mrs. Kennedy and the family. Do something that reflects the way the community feels.

"Mrs. Kennedy has been a—the only word that comes to mind is 'Great Lady'—the dignity and pride; we have to think of her.

"The decent thing to do is let some time elapse. Then get in contact with the family. Various people have been thinking of things the President—and she—were interested in: cultural, education, interest in young people. Or something to build respect for the law. Set up in his name. Let everybody, everywhere take part."

The voices . . . voices . . . voices:
The bus driver takes you in from the airport: "Ohh, boy," and a long sigh. "This is a sad town, Gentlemen."
Q. "What are people saying?"
A. "It's about all anybody can talk about—what happened. Now the hospital is over there, sir, on the other road, and the Trade Mart right here—where they were gonna have the luncheon."
Downtown on the street: "I'm a native Texan—and I feel the greatest sense of guilt."
The coffee shop: "It's funny, we were sitting right here when we were told the President was killed, and we came back here today. Regardless of your grievance, this man was a hero. A great man, a brilliant man—and in all probability a very, very great President."
A local newspaper reporter: "Sad city? It's pretty well shocked, I'll tell you that. One thing I've noticed, I don't see any more 'Goldwater in 1964' bumper stickers around anymore. There were quite a few. The newspapers, mayor, police been getting calls from all over."
"Guilt? I don't have a feeling of guilt about it. I'm just heartsick. This lunatic fringe we've got here. I think they had something to do with the Adlai Stevenson trouble."
The veteran worldwide reporter for newspapers, magazines, in books: "I've been here since the day of the assassination talking with people, and you ask me what the average person in Dallas is thinking—and I can't tell you."
H. L. Hunt, oilman whom the local press describes as "millionaire ultraconservative," said after the assassination: "Every American, whatever the faith of his views or his political affiliations, suffers a personal loss when a President dies . . . freedom is in a fearful danger when a President dies by violence."
Said Allan Maley, secretary-treasurer of the Dallas AFL-CIO Council: "This is no time to try to place blame . . . but it is high time for all of us to take a long, hard look at our city. Statements that I made following the assault on Ambassador Stevenson have been made to appear prophetic.
"There is no use beating around the bush. Dallas is a sick city. There are powerful leaders who have encouraged or condoned or at best remained silent while the preachment of hate helped condition a citizenry to support the most reactionary sort of political philosophy.
"We have been taught that we should hate . . . Dallas has become the mecca for political and social extremists, some sin-

cere, some demented, and some just plain hoodlums. To their credit, most of the leaders finally recognize the terrible offspring they have sired. But truly, another Frankenstein has lost control of his monster . . . I feel that it will take years for Dallas to recover."

Dallas is said to have one of the highest murder rates. It had 103 murders last year. The police force has been called a good one. A President, a patrolman, and an alleged assassin were murdered here on the same violent weekend, in a connected chain of assassination, attempted arrest, and self-appointed execution.

The widow of patrolman J. D. Tippit stands to collect $225 a month in pension money, half to her and half to the three children. A grateful world has so far given the Tippit widow and children more than $50,000.

One man said the city was "completely stunned and shocked and unanimously grieved at the tragic thing that happened—no one feels unique in grief but some probably feel more sorrowful because it happened here."

The Mayor, after the violent weekend, said: "Now is the time for all of us to come to our senses . . . I ask only that the world recognize and appreciate the burden Dallas bears."

By midweek, there were many messages appreciating and unappreciating. Thousands. One was from the editor of the Fort Worth *Press* on his front page: "If there are any two hard-hitting rivals in the country they are Fort Worth and Dallas. . . .

"We now come to the defense of our neighbor, for it is a vibrant, strong, patriotic American city. And the good people who live there are being crucified . . . Dallas has its crackpots. So have all cities.

"It is a shame which the people of Dallas feel deeply . . . [it] could have happened in any city in America, in any parade."

The Chicago *Tribune* said the Dallas police were being subjected to unjust censure, that the city had received much unjust criticism because of the accident of a strike by two madmen: "It would be shameful if the good name of the city were stained by events which could not have been foreseen, and hence, controlled."

At the Monday memorial service at Austin, in front of the capitol, Judge W. A. Morrison, of the State Court of Criminal Appeals, in a eulogy said: "We hang our heads in shame because he was assassinated in our Lone Star State. . . .

"We must rid ourselves, each of us, of all racial bigotry. We must school ourselves to look at and treat every man with complete equality. . . .

"From this day forward, Texans must be known as progressive thinkers, just as was President Kennedy. We must abandon the ways of the old South just as surely as we must continue our battle against communism. There shall hereafter be no place or welcome in the Lone Star State for those of either the extreme right or extreme left."

Silver spangles of Christmas twinkle in the bright Texas sunlight on Commerce Street in Dallas. The decorations hang high over the streets in multiple garlands, over the flashing incandescence and neon lights of the "Zoo Bar," beside the magnificent concave glass expanse of the Statler-Hilton, alongside the moving-sign lights of "Victor's Lounge, Entertainment Nightly," and the "Pla-mor Recreation Club."

They were there on the Monday of national mourning, with the flags at half-staff curling smartly on top of the high hotels. The sign in the toy-store window down below said neatly: "In respect to our late President, Neiman-Marcus Co. will be closed Monday, Nov. 25." Inside the door sat baby dolls in cradles.

There were fluffy dogs and pandas sitting audaciously on the floor in their locked-up state—waiting for kids. It made a stranger think of children, and of a little girl named Caroline in a picture some time back kissing and biting a fatherly hand as they strode along.

Captain Will Fritz of the Dallas police (below left) declared on Saturday that the case was "cinched." The affidavit charging Oswald with the crime is displayed (below right) by an officer, and two policemen stand outside the Homicide Bureau, guarding the prisoner against any possible harm.

The assassin's 6.5 mm. rifle is held aloft for the press at Dallas Police Headquarters, right.

Dallas: Saturday

While the rest of the world was involved with its private thoughts, the Dallas police proceeded with the case of Lee Harvey Oswald. The evidence against him was impressive: ballistics tests proved that the rifle bearing Oswald's prints was the murder weapon; an order, in Oswald's handwriting, showed he had purchased the rifle from a mail-order house; paraffin tests for gunpowder on Oswald's hands were "positive." He had, of course, been in the building from which the shots were fired, at the time they were fired. The case against Lee Harvey Oswald, that Saturday, looked air-tight. Yet the handling of the case by the Dallas police—the assumption of Oswald's guilt, the long hours of grilling without legal counsel, the omnipresent glare of television cameras, the hectic atmosphere of police headquarters—all gave witnesses an uneasy feeling about the due process of law in Dallas.

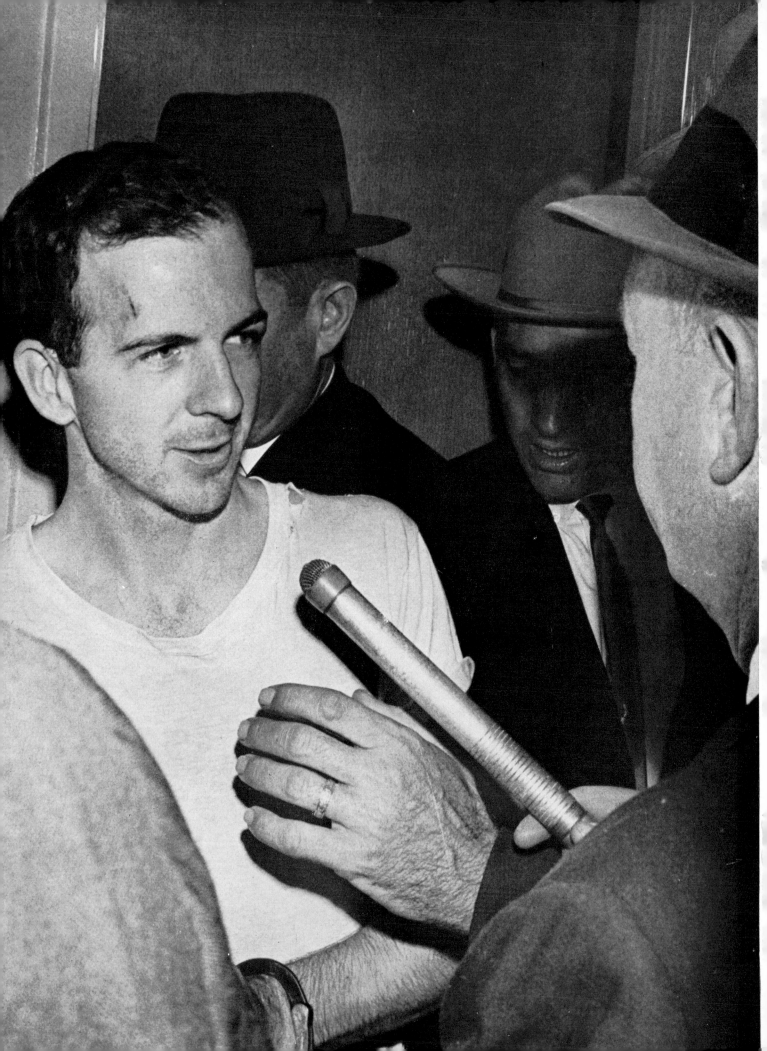

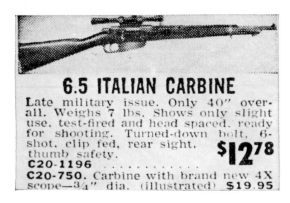

6.5 ITALIAN CARBINE
Late military issue. Only 40" over-
all. Weighs 7 lbs. Shows only slight
use, test-fired and head spaced, ready
for shooting. Turned-down bolt, 6-
shot, clip fed, rear sight,
thumb safety.   **$12⁷⁸**
C20-1196 . . . .
C20-750. Carbine with brand new 4X
scope—¾" dia. (illustrated) $19.95

New bits of evidence concerning
Oswald were turned up quickly on Saturday.
The catalogue advertisement, left,
showed the rifle he had ordered
from a Chicago mail-order house—the
same type used to kill the
President. A letter to Governor Connally,
written by Oswald in 1962,
demanded that the young man's
undesirable discharge from the
Marines be reconsidered.

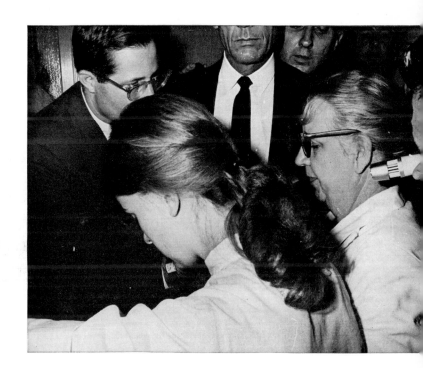

Lee Harvey Oswald

Lee Harvey Oswald—called innocent by his mother and his wife, above, and
guilty by most others—denied everything. Oswald was born in 1939 in New
Orleans, lived for a time in New York, where he was a chronic truant and,
according to a school psychiatrist's report, a "potentially dangerous" schizo-
phrenic. He entered high school near Dallas, and withdrew after twenty-
three days to join the Marines. After three years of military service, where he
earned a marksman's medal and two courts-martial, Oswald traveled to
Moscow in 1959, and tried to renounce his American citizenship. He returned to America with the help of—and a loan from—the U.S. Government
in 1962, bringing a Russian wife. He preached Marxism and once, in New
Orleans, gained notoriety by distributing pro-Castro leaflets. But Lee, according to his mother, "was a good boy."

That Was the Week That Was

That Was the Week That Was, a satirical television program broadcast over Britain's BBC every Saturday evening, had frequently singled out John Kennedy as its target. But, on November 23, there was a different atmosphere in the studio. Here is an excerpt:

DAVID FROST: The reason why the shock was so great, why when one heard the news last night one felt suddenly so empty, was because it was the most unexpected piece of news one could possibly imagine. It was the least likely thing to happen in the whole world. If anyone else had died—Sir Winston Churchill, de Gaulle, Khrushchev—it would have been something that somehow we could have understood and even perhaps accepted. But that Kennedy should go, well, we just didn't believe in assassination any more, not in the civilized world anyway.

ROY KINNEAR: When Kennedy was elected three years ago, it was as if we'd all been given some gigantic miraculous present. Suddenly over there in Washington was this amazing man who seemed so utterly right for the job in every way that we took him completely for granted. Whenever we thought about the world, we had that warm image at the back of our minds of a man who would keep everything on the rails. Now suddenly that present has been taken away from us when we thought we had still five more years before we need start worrying again.

KENNETH COPE: When the news came through just before eight o'clock last night, more than a thousand people all over London caught buses or tube trains, took taxis, drove or walked to the American Embassy in Grosvenor Square. They had to do something.

WILLIAM RUSHTON: When Kennedy was picked to be the Democratic candidate for the Presidency in 1960, the general opinion was that Kennedy was too perfect, too good to be true, a sort of public relations officer's ideal American: the film-star image, the beautiful wife, the great speeches with easy quotations from Burke and Shakespeare, the ice-cold efficiency, respect for the facts. But there was the homely, all-American humanity of the man when he went out on his family boating picnics. His wife was down at one end of the boat eating the *pâté de foie gras,* he was sitting quite happily in the bow of the boat knocking back the peanut butter sandwiches.

LANCE PERCIVAL: But once Kennedy was in office, the dream came true. Behind the rocking chair and the cultural evenings at the White House and Caroline's pony and the parties in Bobby's swimming pool, behind the trappings of the image, was the first Western politician to make politics a respectable profession for thirty years, to make it once again the highest of the professions and not just a fabric of fraud and sham. He was simply and superlatively a man of his age, who understood his age, who put all his own energy and the best brains of his country into solving its problems and who ended up in more cases than not by doing the right thing at the right time because he'd gone about it in the right way.

DAVID FROST: Yesterday one man died, today in America sixty lost their lives in a fire. Yet somehow it is the ONE that matters. Even in death, it seems, we're not equal. Death is not the great leveler. Death reveals the eminent.

ROBERT LANG: How little true it is that all power tends to corrupt and absolute power corrupts absolutely. It would be closer to the truth to say that such power transforms, elevates, even purifies its holder. At the assumption of so terrible a burden, even as it marks out its bearer as a man forever apart, at the same time it gives him the strength to live it.

BERNARD LEVIN: In the world of today neither grief nor shock can be permitted to create an interregnum in the citadels of power. And such is the pace at which the modern world moves that even before the mourning is over, indeed, before it has begun, we must begin to think not of the past but of the future.

What, then, can be read of the future with President Johnson? For the time has long since gone by when the responsibility of the President of the United States was confined to the people of that country alone.

I believe that this now-global responsibility has fallen into good hands. The contrast between President Johnson and his predecessors is more obvious than important. Johnson, unlike Kennedy, is not an intellectual, but then neither was Truman. Johnson is provincial where Kennedy was metropolitan, but his years as leader of the Senate gave him a knowledge, understanding, and control of the realities of power in politics, almost as sophisticated as that of Roosevelt. Johnson, in the inevitable isolation of the Vice Presidency, has had no direct power to exercise, yet Kennedy, unlike Roosevelt, took his deputy fully into his confidence, and shared with him the results of his decisions, if not their making. President Johnson will bring to the awful responsibility of his office qualities and a record that offer promise that he will be more than merely the best available shadow of the light that failed.

Nor is there any reason to fear that the thaw in the frozen attitudes of East-West relations will be seriously endangered, let alone reversed by President Johnson's accession. His incomparable political shrewdness, the clarity and firmness of the lines which President Kennedy had drawn on the charts and policy into the future, the team of younger men that he has inherited— these will combine to ensure continuity in those aspects of American policy which are of such direct concern to us all. And the ambassadorial mission he undertook for the then fledgling President a few weeks after Kennedy had been elected, took him through Western Europe, including Britain, and wherever he went he made a good impression which will stand him in good stead now.

Nobody tonight can wish more fervently than President Johnson himself that this dreadful opportunity had not fallen upon him. But since it has, we, citizens of the Alliance he now leads, have the right to hope for much from his leadership and a duty to wish him well with all our hearts. I think those hopes and wishes will not be disappointed.

A poet once hymned an earlier, narrower moment of crisis in the life of the United States. How much more bitterly relevant are Longfellow's words today:

> *Sail on, oh ship of State.*
> *Sail on, oh Union strong and great.*
> *Humanity with all its fears,*
> *With all the hopes of future years,*
> *Is hanging on thy fate.*

DAVID FROST: The tragedy of John Kennedy's death is not that the liberal movements of history that he led will cease, it is that their focus may become blurred and that the gathering momentum may be lost.

That is the aftermath of Dallas, November 22.

It is a time for private thoughts.

SUNDAY

24

NOV. 1963

As Sunday morning dawned in Washington, Saturday's rain had given way to chilly sunshine. A pensive quiet hung over the nation's capital. Inside the White House, John Fitzgerald Kennedy's body lay in the flag-draped coffin in the East Room, as Abraham Lincoln's had lain a century earlier, awaiting the horse-drawn caisson that would carry it to the Capitol rotunda. John F. Kennedy, Jr., not quite three years old, slept peacefully, his young mind unpossessed by what had happened. Outside, a few citizens, somber-faced, had already taken positions from which to watch the procession. Many others moved along Washington streets toward early church services. In his Spring Valley home President Lyndon B. Johnson, awake to the harsh reality of new responsibilities, arose for a ten o'clock conference with John A. McCone and McGeorge Bundy before going to church.

The unretarded earth rolled eastward, and dawn reached Dallas, Texas. There, too, it was sunny; there, too, it was chilly and quiet. Inside the Dallas city prison, Lee Harvey Oswald, now declared by Dallas police to be the undoubted assassin, awaited an armored car assigned to transfer him to the county jail. He had been allowed to sleep that night after hour upon hour of police interrogation. He still had admitted nothing, had seen no legal counsel. At the fatal curve in downtown Dallas, a trickle of curious people came early to stare at the spot where the incredible thing had happened; across the street, in a little park, the sun glinted on floral wreaths brought the day before by grieving groups and individuals. As the morning wore on, church bells slowly tolled in Washington and Dallas and across the nation; millions went to pray. Other millions, tired and depressed by the strain of a weekend already tragic beyond expression, awoke late, dawdled listlessly over breakfast, turned on television sets and radios with a kind of hopeless attentiveness. It promised to be a day of solemn ritual, of quiet mourning and sad reflection.

It turned out to be a great deal more than that.

At one o'clock on Sunday afternoon Jacqueline Kennedy appeared at the north portico of the White House, dressed all in unaccustomed black, to watch her husband's last departure from the presidential mansion. Caroline and John, Jr., in light blue coats, stood one on either side of her as the coffin was placed in position by the pallbearers.

Last departure

No other presidential couple in American history did more to identify themselves with the White House than John and Jacqueline Kennedy. Both of them—and especially Jacqueline—saw it as far more than the presidential mansion, their home during his years in office. They saw it as a truly national shrine, a place for Americans to visit with pleasure and gather a sense, as Mrs. Kennedy herself put it, "that many First Families loved this house, and that each and every one left something of themselves behind in it." That, of course, was the point of her continuous efforts to restore to the Executive Mansion pieces of furniture, paintings, and décor that had been part of the living *ambiance* of former Presidents and First Ladies. There was thus a special poignancy to the moment when Jacqueline Kennedy and John F. Kennedy left the White House together for the last time.

State flags dipped in homage as the cortege left the White House grounds.

To the Capitol

The procession to the Capitol, watched by hundreds of thousands lining the route, was traditional in style and reminiscent of earlier ones: Franklin D. Roosevelt's in 1945—which used the same caisson; Garfield's in 1881; Lincoln's in 1865. Indeed, a newspaper account written in April, 1865, might have been written on this day in 1963: "The procession which escorted the body from the White House to the Capitol was one of the most imposing ever seen in Washington . . . The avenue was cleared the whole length . . . The sound of muffled drums was heard, and the procession, with a slow and measured tread, moved from the home of mourning on its mission with the remains of the illustrious dead. Despite the enormous crowd the silence was profound."

Above, the caisson moves up
Pennsylvania Avenue, escorted
by an honor guard drawn
from all the Armed Forces.
Right: their drums muted in
accordance with ancient
custom, a corps of drummers
sets a slow pace.

As the cortege drew up before the east front of the Capitol, an indifferent wind whipped the flag at half-staff on the roof. It ruffled the edges of the flag draped over the coffin, and the head pallbearer stepped forward to tuck them down. The coffin was unlashed, and the pallbearers lifted their burden. From the black limousines Mrs. Kennedy, her children, her brother-in-law Robert, the Attorney General, and the rest of the government party descended and stood silent for a moment. It was time to go in.

The steps were long for the pallbearers,
but they did not falter. The
children mounted easily behind them,
their hands grasped by their mother.
In the rotunda (opposite) the casket was
silently lowered onto Lincoln's catafalque.

In the rotunda

The magnificent rotunda of the Capitol, with its
friezes and great paintings commemorating dra-
matic moments in the American past, was a fitting
place for the body of John F. Kennedy to lie in
state. His sense of the value of history in stimulat-
ing men to noble efforts was acute. There was also
a centennial note to this occasion: almost exactly
one hundred years before, late in 1863, the present soaring dome over the rotunda had been com-
pleted, replacing one only half as high. It was begun
in 1856, and despite the economic strain of the
Civil War, Lincoln had insisted that the work go
on as a symbol of the permanence of the Union.

Three speakers eulogized the dead
President during the brief
ceremony in the rotunda: Senate
Majority Leader Mike Mansfield;
Speaker of the House John W. McCormack;
and Chief Justice Earl Warren.
The picture opposite gives a general
view during the eulogies.
Above, members of the Kennedy
family: Robert Kennedy; Peter Lawford
with his daughter Sydney;
his wife, Patricia Kennedy Lawford;
Caroline and her mother.

A time to remember

Nothing etched itself so sharply on
the minds of all those who watched,
in the rotunda and on television, as
the moment when Jacqueline
Kennedy and her daughter went to the
bier and knelt beside it. The
young widow kissed the flag; the
child reached under it to touch her
father's coffin. Both the view from
high in the rotunda (left) and
that of the spectators on the floor
(above) record the same moment—one
not easily forgotten in the annals of
four days of national tragedy.

Her tears never fell

Jacqueline Bouvier Kennedy entered the great rotunda of the Capitol at 1:58 P.M. EST. She left twenty-two minutes later, her head erect, her tears still unshed. She had watched intently while the uniformed bearers gently placed the flag-covered casket of her martyred husband on the same catafalque on which had rested, in the same place, the bodies of three other Presidents who had died the same way. She touched the black lace which covered her dark hair. She bent to say something to her children, five-year-old Caroline, and John, Jr., who would be three on the day of his father's funeral. A naval aide relieved her of John, who was getting wriggly. Caroline remained at her mother's right hand. Former President Harry Truman watched sympathetically. The new President, Lyndon B. Johnson, was five paces away. Standing beside Caroline was the dead man's brother, Attorney General Robert F. Kennedy. All around the great room with its soaring vault stood the great of this and other lands—congressmen, cabinet officers, justices of the Supreme Court, ambassadors.

Jacqueline Kennedy had stood on the White House porch with her children for nearly five minutes waiting for her husband's last ride to the Capitol to get under way. She stood without flinching. Now she had to stand and wait some more.

The first of the speeches started at 2:02 P.M. EST. The face she turned toward the man who was talking was the classic mask of tragedy. There was the shine of tears in her eyes, but her lips never trembled. Once the long eyelashes drooped. For an instant her eyes closed, her shoulders sagged. The moment passed. She bent her head to say something to Caroline. Then she turned her gaze again on the speaker. He was telling how, in Dallas on Friday, she took a ring from her finger and placed it in her dying husband's hands. Her gaze went to the casket reposing beneath the great dome on the ancient catafalque. She leaned a little in the direction of her gaze.

The speaker stopped. She thanked him with the ghost of a smile. Another speaker started his remarks. Caroline's mother bent her head slightly and whispered to the little girl. She did it gravely, without expression. A third speaker, the last, began his tribute to the slain President. Midway in his remarks the soldierly figure of Jacqueline Bouvier Kennedy swayed again. Again no one near her noticed. Again the moment passed. She lifted her eyes to the summit of the dome and closed them briefly. Her shoulders firmed again. The words of the speaker came to an end.

Bobby Kennedy whispered something. Soldiers carried the red, white, and blue wreath of President Johnson to the casket. Jacqueline took the hand of her daughter and together they walked fifteen paces to the catafalque. They knelt together at the casket. The time was 2:19 P.M. EST. Mother and daughter rose and retraced the fifteen agonizing steps. All the time the eyes of television had been watching. They were still watching as a beautiful and brave woman and her little daughter walked out into the world again.

Joseph L. Myler, UPI Correspondent

Opposite: The Kennedy family leaves the Capitol after the ceremony.

Another act of violence

The killing of Lee Harvey Oswald, President Kennedy's alleged assassin, while actually in the hands of the Dallas police was undoubtedly the most astonishing sequence ever projected, live, to a television audience—one that included many million viewers. The numbered pictures on these two pages, taken from UPI Newsfilm, show what they saw as police attempted to transfer Oswald from the city prison to the county jail on that fateful Sunday morning.

1. At 11:19 A.M., Dallas time, detectives take Oswald in an elevator from his upper floor cell to the basement of the city prison.

2. Emerging from the elevator, Oswald is led toward the armored car.

5. As Oswald turns toward the waiting vehicle, a burly form plunges forward, arm outstretched.

6. The man points a gun at Oswald . . .

3. He passes reporters and other onlookers.

4. Suddenly the figure of a man (wearing hat) enters the scene at extreme right.

7. . . . drives it into his ribs and fires one shot. Oswald slumps, while a policeman who has seen the assailant shouts, "Jack, you son of a bitch!"

8. Oswald has fallen from sight, and the police start to react.

Overleaf: Oswald grimaces with pain as the bullet rips through his viscera.

A death heavy with irony

The accused assassin of President Kennedy was gunned down as crowds formed in Washington to watch the removal of the President's body from White House to Capitol. Word of this new act of violence spread rapidly, adding a note of incredulous shock to the mood of mourning. Within an hour of Oswald's death, Dallas homicide chief Will Fritz announced grimly that the case of the presidential assassination was now "closed"—a word soon to be disputed in Washington and across the country. One thing was certain, however: Oswald's lips, from which no word of confession had yet come, were now closed. The Dallas police said evidence against him was "airtight."

Astounded Dallas detectives immediately wrestled the assailant to the floor and seized his gun (left), while Oswald, writhing in pain, was hastily laid on a stretcher and shoved into an ambulance (above). He was rushed to an emergency room at Parkland Hospital, a few feet from where President Kennedy had been declared dead two days earlier. At 1:07 P.M., Oswald was himself dead from massive internal bleeding (right).

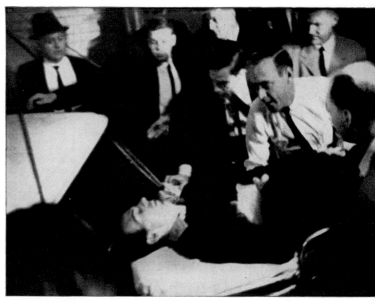

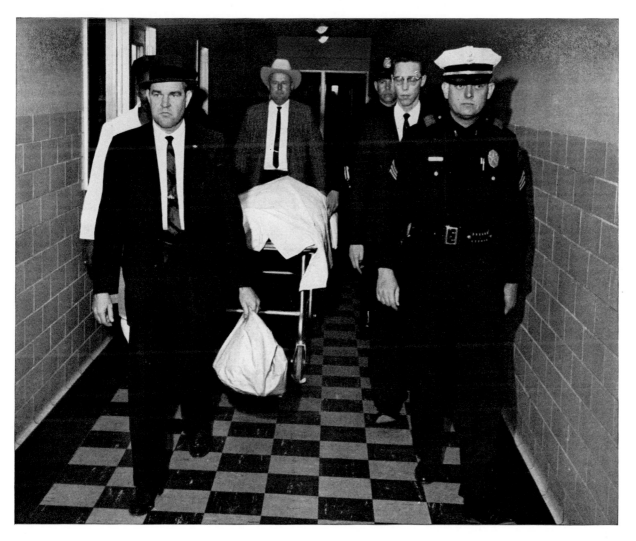

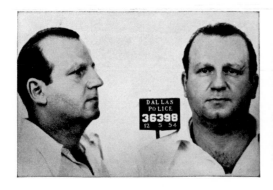

The Dallas police had no trouble identifying the man who had killed Oswald. He was an old acquaintance. Jack Ruby, fifty-two years of age, was the proprietor of a popular Dallas strip-tease joint called the Carousel (right). His "mug shot" (above) was already in Dallas police files, with a record of several arrests—twice for carrying a concealed weapon.

One-man vigilante

Jack Ruby, who was immediately clapped behind bars by Dallas police, and shortly thereafter charged with murder, appeared to be a type not unfamiliar in the precincts of big city police headquarters. He was known as a flashy dresser—"strictly Broadway," one reporter said—who put great emphasis on what he called "class." Acquaintances said he courted a reputation as a sport with the strippers in his club, where he also liked to be impresario at "amateur nights," and ran a kind of strip-tease school. Reports from Chicago, whence Ruby had come to Texas in 1948, revealed a background of small-time gambling, gate-crashing, barroom brawling; in Dallas he was proud of being a do-it-yourself bouncer in his own club. He was always ready to glad-hand policemen, or give them one on the house; he not only treated them but admired them. On Sunday morning he had been able to get into the city prison as an almost unnoticed figure, just one of the boys. Later, his sister told reporters that his motive for killing Oswald must have been his intense admiration for Kennedy.

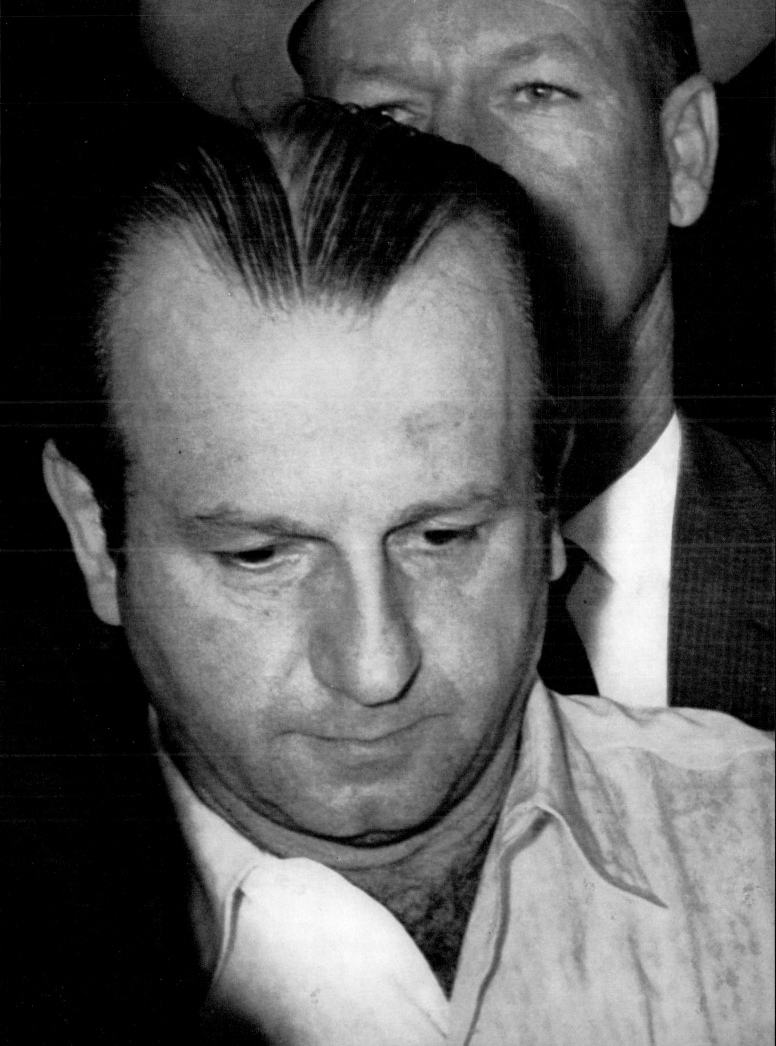

The homage
of the people

There was something deeply impressive about the
great crowds that filed quietly through the Capitol
rotunda Sunday afternoon, and on through the
long, cold night. It was not their sheer mass, though
estimates were that something like 250,000 had
passed the bier by morning. Nor was it any intense
expression of emotion: the faces picked up recur-
rently by the television cameras, as they turned to
look at the flag-covered coffin, seldom showed tears,
and most had a kind of blankness. It was the way
they kept coming, and the stubborn patience with
which they shuffled along the pavement outside—
for at times the line of waiting mourners was two
miles long, and it took six to eight hours to reach
the rotunda. They knew in advance that there
would not be much to see: only the silent coffin and
its silent and motionless guard of honor. Still they
came, as if it were an indispensable personal ges-
ture. They were, in great majority, ordinary people.
Now and then a person of importance would appear—John Glenn, the astronaut; President Kennedy's mother; President de Valera of Ireland.

All through the night crowds flocked to the Capitol, in a spontaneous demonstration the likes of which Washington had seldom, if ever, witnessed. Shortly after nine o'clock Mrs. Kennedy suddenly appeared unannounced, with her brother-in-law Robert, knelt beside the coffin momentarily, then departed. She and the dead President's brother walked for some blocks, almost unremarked by the thousands of people they passed, before getting back into a limousine and vanishing into the night.

MONDAY

25

NOV. 1963

At a few minutes before seven, a cloudless sun rose over the eastern shore of the Potomac, presaging a clear, cold day. In Washington every dawn singles out the gilded peak of the Capitol dome on its high hill for first light. But on this particular morning early glints fell on long files of citizens who had stood in line through the night and were still waiting to pass the bier of the President in the rotunda. By nine o'clock the sum of men and women who had made their pilgrimage here during the past eighteen hours of the lying-in-state, often with children in their arms, had reached the astounding total of 250,000. Then the bronze doors were closed in preparation for the final day—the solemn ceremonies in which, after so much voice of individual and private grief, the nation as a whole was to offer final homage to its fallen leader.

"He belongs to the country," Jacqueline Kennedy had said, expressing her wish to have the President laid to rest in the National Cemetery at Arlington rather than in the family plot in Massachusetts. More than that: he belonged to the world. Monarchs, presidents, chancellors, prime ministers, had flooded into Washington from five continents the day before, and now stood waiting at the White House at the approach of noon, when all bells tolled, for the moment when king and commissar, Frenchman and Ethiopian, South American and Asian, would alike follow John F. Kennedy's black caisson to the funeral on foot.

But while this austere procession from around the globe was in one sense the summit of that clear, cold day, there were other sights and sounds no less poignant, to be etched immemorably on the minds of the million people who lined the route and the scores of millions who followed it by television: the straining shoulders of the nine servicemen carrying their flag-draped burden down the Capitol steps; the rearing of a riderless black horse, as if protesting the loss of his chieftain; the salute of a little boy; the folding of a flag; and always, always, the throb of muffled drums in slow cadence.

And perhaps the most eloquent single fact about that day, when all the world was watching, was that shortly before the noonday tolled and the requiem mass was to begin, the number of television viewers dropped abruptly. Countless Americans across the land—how many millions no one will ever know—had switched off their sets and gone in silence to their own churches and temples to pray.

Hail to the Chief

It was 10:50 A.M. on Monday, and the ceremony of Sunday was reversed as the nine men from the five armed services who had borne the President into the Capitol carried him down the long steps for his last journey. The Navy band that saluted his entrance struck up for his departure the presidential song, "Hail to the Chief," and the stately Navy hymn "Eternal Father, Strong to Save." The national colors and the President's flag that had stood by his bier accompanied him once more. Mrs. Kennedy stands at left, between her husband's brothers, Robert and Edward. On pages 102–103, members of the family watch as the casket is loaded onto the caisson.

"O hear us when we cry to Thee
 For those in peril on the sea."
So runs the refrain of the Navy hymn
played as the President was carried
to the caisson. He knew the words from
his war service. Navy men have known
them since the Civil War,
when the hymn was composed.

The caisson rolls

The casket is placed upon the gun carriage (above), to begin its processional across the city, past the White House to St. Matthew's Cathedral and then to Arlington. Though among great nations ours has been perhaps the least bent upon panoply and ceremony, a tradition of dignity on high state occasions has persevered.

Six gray-white horses, three of them riderless, draw the body from Capitol to cathedral. Massed companies of officers and men preceded it; a new President followed it.

Marche funèbre

After the bands turned up Fifteenth Street, nearing the White House, they struck up Frédéric Chopin's Funeral March, and its reverberations sounded through the grounds of the Executive Mansion as the clanking cortege approached. As the blast of slow trumpets died away, the cortege stopped outside the White House while the family and the dignitaries of the world left their automobiles and assembled behind the caisson to walk to St. Matthew's Cathedral. In the photograph above, the head of the procession emerges from the White House drive. Below, Black Jack, the uneasy, riderless horse that walked in the parade as the symbol of a lost leader, is led behind the casket.

Boots are reversed in Black Jack's stirrups to mark the death of the rider (right). At left, a sailor weeps.

Captains and kings

Behind members of the Kennedy family (below), walking in back of the casket, came the world's great. Crowned heads (Baudouin of Belgium, center; Frederika of Greece on his right; Haile Selassie of Ethiopia on his left) were dominated in their walk from White House to cathedral by the magisterial presence of President de Gaulle of France, wearing the simple khaki uniform that recalled his service in two world wars. At his right, President Lübke of West Germany; close behind the Greek queen, Chancellor Erhard from Bonn; at right in the front row, the Presidents of the Philippines (next to Haile Selassie) and the Korean Republic. Some two hundred dignitaries of high rank followed them—intermixed with Secret Service agents and bodyguards galore.

Overleaf: Huge throngs stood quiet as the caisson rumbled by,
followed by the riderless horse, the chief mourners,
and a broad assemblage of the world's great and titled leaders.

Requiem

"O God, who alone art ever merciful in sparing of punishment, humbly we pray Thee on behalf of the soul of Thy servant, John Fitzgerald Kennedy. . . ." As the body faces the altar of St. Matthew's Cathedral, Richard Cardinal Cushing (who had also officiated at John Kennedy's wedding and spoken at his Inaugural) celebrates the pontifical requiem mass. Below, he blesses the casket outside the cathedral.

A little soldier's salute

Washington, Nov. 25 (UPI) — A little boy at his grieving mother's side saluted the passing casket.

And in that moment, he suddenly became the brave soldier his father would have wanted him to be on this day, of all days.

For today, John F. Kennedy, Jr., turned three.

His world was strangely different, in little ways a child notices but does not understand.

Where was his daddy? The tall man with the laughing blue eyes who had a big desk and saw lots of important people and stooped to spank him good-naturedly and took him on helicopter rides and called him "John-John."

This was supposed to be the day of The Party. The cake with three candles to blow out, the friends singing boisterous "Happy Birthdays," the gifts.

But home, the White House, was quiet. Some of the furniture was gone. And the soldiers outside, whose salutes he delighted in trying to return with one of his own, looked different. They didn't glance down at him and sneak a wink or a smile today. Their commands barked, their rifles clattered.

Secret Service agents came and led John-John and his sister out to the north portico. Mrs. Kennedy, dressed all in black, met them at the door and took them to a limousine. Then she walked back up in line with their uncles, Attorney General Robert F. Kennedy and Senator Edward Kennedy, and the slow, sad march to church began.

President and Mrs. Johnson and a host of aides and security agents followed Mrs. Kennedy on foot. John-John and Caroline rode in the car behind them.

A half-mile later, in front of St. Matthew's Cathedral, the parade stopped. John-John and Caroline were brought around to join their mother.

The little boy looked around bewildered and started crying. His mother spoke to him softly, and he stopped.

They walked up the steps of the cathedral, and there waiting was Richard Cardinal Cushing of Boston. John-John seemed awed by the tall, craggy-faced man towering above him, wearing a white, two-pointed miter and black vestments.

Mrs. Kennedy, holding each of her children by the hand, walked in and down the aisle to their seats.

John-John grew restless during the mass. Someone picked a small book— *The Church Today—Growth or Decline*—from the literature rack at the rear of the cathedral and gave it to the boy to occupy him. He still clasped it in his hand when he left the church with his mother and sister.

They stood waiting at the bottom of the steps. Pallbearers appeared at the door with the flag-draped casket, and as it came slowly down toward them, Mrs. Kennedy leaned down and whispered to her son.

He stood apart, straightened stiffly, and raised his hand in salute as the casket passed.

Robert M. Andrews, UPI Correspondent

Resuming the march
after the service, the
head of the column and
the red-coated Marine band
approach the shrine
of another martyred
President

In the presence of Lincoln

No memorial in the nation's capital is more nobly sited than that to Abraham Lincoln. At the plaza around the monument the cortege turned and continued over the Arlington Memorial Bridge across the Potomac (above) to the National Cemetery on the broad rise beyond. From the open hall along the way, the great seated figure of Lincoln carved by Daniel Chester French has looked out over the years upon all those who come from the city's heart. On this day, many marchers and dignitaries were seen to look upward to the brooding head of stone, just before they swung to the right. The band fell silent as it rounded the shrine; only the drums were heard.

Haven of heroes

Anyone who has served with honor in America's armed forces is entitled to burial at Arlington, and today some 120,000 veterans (sometimes with members of their families) lie there on the slope facing the capital city and the Lincoln Memorial—the famous and obscure alike under long lines of headstones. The ceremonial horses drawing this veteran's body uphill, with the still-restless black charger behind them, have done similar duty many times before. But now the military formations that preceded them across the bridge have moved to the side at parade rest. Soon the drums will cease.

Three of John F. Kennedy's
military chiefs, Generals Maxwell
Taylor (left), Curtis LeMay
of the Air Force (center), and
David M. Shoup of the
Marines, are among
those to pay last respects.

Dust to dust

When the body was brought to its last resting place,
the massed band that had played President Kennedy so movingly through the streets of the capital
finally struck up the national anthem. All faces remained absorbed and tense while there was a flyover
of fifty jet planes, one for each state of the republic,
plus Air Force One, the President's personal jet,
which flew over alone. Then Cardinal Cushing said
a prayer, and the presidential salute of twenty-one
guns reverberated from the hills.

The watchers

One man who had been intimately involved with the tragic beginning of the four days—UPI White House correspondent Merriman Smith—was on hand as the ceremonies at Arlington drew to a close. He wrote: "America buried John Fitzgerald Kennedy on Arlington's green slopes today, consigning his body to the land he loved and his soul to the God he worshipped . . . Joining the family and all America in its grief were kings, presidents, ministers and princes from nearly every country of the world, communist as well as free, from Charles de Gaulle of France to Anastas Mikoyan of Russia." Shown below are some of those leaders: De Gaulle, Haile Selassie, and President Macapagal of the Philippines, German Chancellor Erhard (behind Selassie), and French Foreign Minister Couve de Murville, behind Erhard and beside Franklin D. Roosevelt, Jr.

Standing beside the President's
widow at Arlington are his
brother, mother, and sister.

After three final salvos of rifle fire and the playing of "Taps," servicemen who had accompanied the body through its transit still rigidly hold the flag that covered it. A moment later, it was properly folded and presented to the President's widow.

Folding the colors

For many of the millions around the world who shared the four days November 22–25, there could have been no more moving moment than that in which the colors that had covered the lost President ever since his return from Dallas were quietly placed in the hands of his grieving wife. Though America is a land with little ceremony, there could hardly have been a more poignant one than this. Afterward, the President's lady and his brother quietly left the place of burial, hand in hand, looking up as they did so to the historic mansion of General Robert E. Lee (overleaf) that was illuminated through the night—a backdrop to the flowers at the grave.

FOR THE RECORD

The following pages present a selection of official documents, public statements, private messages, and other records bearing on the death and funeral of President Kennedy.

The undelivered speech

These were President Kennedy's last official words—the conclusion of the speech he was to have delivered in Dallas.

America today is stronger than ever before. Our adversaries have not abandoned their ambitions—our dangers have not diminished—our vigilance cannot be relaxed. But now we have the military, the scientific and the economic strength to do whatever must be done for the preservation and promotion of freedom.

That strength will never be used in pursuit of aggressive ambitions—it will always be used in pursuit of peace. It will never be used to promote provocations—it will always be used to promote the peaceful settlement of disputes.

We in this country, in this generation, are—by destiny rather than choice —the watchmen on the walls of world freedom. We ask, therefore, that we may be worthy of our power and responsibility—that we may exercise our strength with wisdom and restraint—and that we may achieve in our time and for all time the ancient vision of peace on earth, good will toward men. That must always be our goal—and the righteousness of our cause must always underlie our strength. For as was written long ago: "Except the Lord keep the city, the watchman waketh but in vain."

The eulogies in the rotunda

The following eulogies were delivered in the rotunda of the Capitol on Sunday, November 24, by Senator Mike Mansfield of Montana, Majority Leader of the Senate; Earl Warren, Chief Justice of the United States; and John W. McCormack of Massachusetts, Speaker of the House of Representatives.

BY SENATOR MANSFIELD

There was a sound of laughter; in a moment, it was no more. And so she took a ring from her finger and placed it in his hands.

There was a wit in a man neither young nor old, but a wit full of an old man's wisdom and of a child's wisdom, and then, in a moment it was no more. And so she took a ring from her finger and placed it in his hands.

There was a man marked with the scars of his love of country, a body active with the surge of a life far, far from spent and, in a moment, it was no more. And so she took a ring from her finger and placed it in his hands.

There was a father with a little boy, a little girl and a joy of each in the other. In a moment it was no more, and so she took a ring from her finger and placed it in his hands.

There was a husband who asked much and gave much, and out of the giving and the asking wove with a woman what could not be broken in life, and in a moment it was no more. And so she took a ring from her finger and placed it in his hands, and kissed him and closed the lid of a coffin.

A piece of each of us died at that moment. Yet, in death he gave of himself to us. He gave us of a good heart from which the laughter came. He gave us of a profound wit, from which a great leadership emerged. He gave us of a kindness and a strength fused into a human courage to seek peace without fear.

He gave us of his love that we, too, in turn, might give. He gave that we might give of ourselves, that we might give to one another until there would be no room, no room at all, for the bigotry, the hatred, prejudice and the arrogance which converged in that moment of horror to strike him down.

In leaving us—these gifts, John Fitzgerald Kennedy, President of the United States, leaves with us. Will we take them, Mr. President? Will we have, now, the sense and the responsibility and the courage to take them?

BY CHIEF JUSTICE WARREN

There are few events in our national life that unite Americans and so touch the heart of all of us as the passing of a President of the United States.

There is nothing that adds shock to our sadness at the assassination of our leader, chosen as he is to embody the ideals of our people, the faith we have in our institutions and our belief in the fatherhood of God and the brotherhood of man.

Such misfortunes have befallen the nation on other occasions, but never more shockingly than two days ago.

We are saddened; we are stunned; we are perplexed.

John Fitzgerald Kennedy, a great and good President, the friend of all men of good will, a believer in the dignity and equality of all human beings, a fighter for justice, and apostle of peace, has been snatched from our midst by the bullet of an assassin. What moved some misguided wretch to do this horrible deed may never be known to us, but we do know that such acts are commonly stimulated by forces of hatred and malevolence, such as today are eating their way into the blood stream of American life. What a price we pay for this fanaticism.

It has been said that the only thing we learn from history is that we do not learn. But surely we can learn if we have the will to do so. Surely there is a lesson to be learned from this tragic event. If we really love this country, if we truly love justice and mercy, if we fervently want to make this nation better for those who are to follow us, we can at least abjure the hatred that consumes people, the false accusations that divide us, and the bitterness that begets violence.

Is it too much to hope that the martyrdom of our beloved President might even soften the hearts of those who would themselves recoil from assassination, but who do not shrink from spreading the venom which kindles thoughts of it in others?

Our nation is bereaved. The whole world is poorer because of his loss. But we can all be better Americans because John Fitzgerald Kennedy has passed our way, because he has been our chosen leader at a time in history when his character, his vision, and his quiet courage have enabled him to chart for us a safe course through the shoals of treacherous seas that encompass the world. And now that he is relieved of the almost superhuman burdens we imposed on him, may he rest in peace.

BY SPEAKER McCORMACK

Any citizen of our beloved country who looks back over its history cannot fail to see that we have been blessed with God's favor beyond most other peoples. At each great crisis in our history we have found a leader able to grasp the helm of state and guide the country through the troubles which beset it. In our earliest days, when our strength and wealth were so limited and our problems so great, Washington and Jefferson appeared to lead our people. Two generations later, when our country was torn in two by a fratricidal war, Abraham Lincoln appeared from the mass of the people as a leader able to reunite the nation.

In more recent times, in the critical days of the depression and the great war forced upon us by fascist aggression, Franklin Delano Roosevelt, later Harry S. Truman appeared on the scene to reorganize the country and lead its revived citizens to victory. Finally, only recently, when the cold war was building up the supreme crisis of a threatened nuclear war capable of destroying everything—and everybody—that our predecessors had so carefully built, and which a liberty-loving world wanted, once again a strong and courageous man appeared ready to lead us.

No country need despair so long as God, in His infinite goodness, continues to provide the nation with leaders able to guide it through the successive crises which seem to be the inevitable fate of any great nation.

Surely no country ever faced more gigantic problems than ours in the last few years, and surely no country could have obtained a more able leader in a time of such crisis. President John Fitzgerald Kennedy possessed all the qualities of greatness. He had deep faith, complete confidence, human sympathy, and broad vision which recognized the true values of freedom, equality, and the brotherhood which have always been the marks of the American political dreams.

He had the bravery and a sense of personal duty which made him willing to face up to the great task of being President in these trying times. He had the warmth and the sense of humanity which made the burden of the task bearable for himself and for his associates, and which made all kinds of diverse peoples and races eager to be associated with him in his task. He had the tenacity and determination to carry each stage of his great work through to its successful conclusion.

Now that our great leader has been taken from us in a cruel death, we are bound to feel shattered and helpless in the face of our loss. This is but natural, but as the first bitter pangs of our incredulous grief begins to pass we must thank God that we were privileged, however briefly, to have had this great man for our President. For he has now taken his place among the great figures of world history.

While this is an occasion of deep sorrow it should be also one of dedication. We must have the determination to unite and carry on the spirit of John Fitzgerald Kennedy for a strengthened America and a future world of peace.

Resolutions of the Congress

The following resolutions were passed on November 25. Senator Everett McKinley Dirksen, Minority Leader of the Senate, delivered his speech in support of the resolution in that body.

BY THE SENATE

Resolved, that the Senate has learned with profound sorrow and deep regret of the tragic death of Honorable John Fitzgerald Kennedy, the late President of the United States, and a former Representative and former Senator from the State of Massachusetts.

Resolved, that in recognition of his illustrious statesmanship, his leadership in national and world affairs, and his distinguished public service to his state and the nation, the presiding officer of the Senate appoint a committee, to consist of all the members of the Senate, to attend the funeral of the late President at noon today.

Resolved, that the Senate hereby tenders its deep sympathy to the members of the family of the late President in their sad bereavement.

Resolved, that the Secretary communicate these resolutions to the House of Representatives and transmit an enrolled copy thereof to the family of the late President.

BY THE HOUSE OF REPRESENTATIVES

Resolved, that the House of Representatives has learned with profound regret and sorrow of the tragic death of the late President of the United States, John Fitzgerald Kennedy, illustrious statesman and leader in the nation and in the world.

Resolved, that as a token of honor and in recognition of his eminent and distinguished public services to the nation and to the world the Speaker shall appoint a committee of 100 members of the House to join a similar committee appointed on the part of the Senate to attend the funeral services of the late President.

Resolved, that the House tenders its deep sympathy to the members of the family of the late President in their sad bereavement.

Resolved, that the sergeant at arms of the House be authorized and directed to take such steps as may be necessary for carrying out the provisions of these resolutions and that the necessary expenses in connection therewith be paid out of the contingent fund of the House.

Resolved, that the clerk communicate these resolutions to the Senate and transmit a copy thereof to the family of the late President.

SENATOR DIRKSEN'S EULOGY

The memory of John Fitzgerald Kennedy lingers in this forum of the people. Here we knew his vigorous tread, his flashing smile, his ready wit, his keen mind, his zest for adventure. Here with quiet grief we mourn his departure. Here we shall remember him best as a colleague whose star of public service is indelibly inscribed on the roll of the United States Senate.

And here the eternal question confronts and confounds us. Why must it be? Why must the life of an amiable, friendly, aggressive young man, moved only by high motives, lighted on his way by high hopes, guided by broad plans, impelled by understanding and vision, be brought to an untimely end and with his labor unfinished.

And why, in a free land, untouched by the heel of dictatorship and oppression, where the humblest citizen may freely utter his grievances, must that life be cut short by an evil instrument, moved by malice, frustration and hate? This is the incredible thing which leaves us bewildered and perplexed.

One moment there is the ecstasy of living when one can hear the treble cries of scampering children over the White House lawn, the pleasure of receiving a Thanksgiving turkey which I presented to him but three days before the evil deed, the pleasure of conversation over many things including his hopes for the future, the exciting fact of sunshine and green grass in late November, the endless stream of citizens coming to the President's house, the strident voice of the city rising from the hum of traffic, the animation of saluting crowds, and then the sudden strangling death rattle of dissolution. Who shall say, save that there is a divinity which shapes our ends and marks our days.

As the tumult and grief subside, as the nation resumes and moves forward, and his own generation measures his works and achievements, what shall we say who knew him well—we in this forum where he spent eight years of his life—we who knew him best not as Mr. President but simply as Jack.

We saw him come to the Senate at age thirty-five. We saw him grow. We saw him rise. We saw him elevated to become the Chief Magistrate of this nation. And we saw him as the leader of both branches of this Republic assembled to deliberate over common problems.

In this moment when death has triumphed, when hearts are chastened, when the spirit reels in sheer bewilderment, what do we say, now that the book of life has been closed?

Let me say what we have always said when he was alive, gay, happy, friendly, ambitious and ready to listen.

He had vision that went beyond our own. His determination to effectuate a test-ban treaty is a living example.

He was his own profile in courage. His unrelenting devotion to equality and civil rights attests that fact.

He was devoted to our system of constitutional government. His attitude toward the separation of church and state looms like a shining example.

He had the great virtue of spiritual grace. If at any moment he may have seemed frustrated over a proposition, it was so transitory. If he showed any sign of petulance, it was so fleeting. There were no souring acids in his spirit. If at any moment, he may have seemed overeager, it was but the reflection of a zealous crusader and missioner who knew where he was going.

If at any moment, he seemed to depart from the covenant which he and his party made with the people, it was only because he believed that accelerated events and circumstances did not always heed the clock and the calendar. If his course sometimes seemed at variance with his own party leaders or with the opposition, it was only because a deep conviction dictated his course.

On the tablets of memory, we who knew him well as a friend and colleague, can well inscribe this sentiment:

Senator John Fitzgerald Kennedy, who became the 35th President of the United States—young, vigorous, aggressive and scholarly—one who estimated the needs of his country and the world and sought to fulfill that need—one who was wedded to peace and vigorously sought this greatest of all goals of mankind—one who sensed how catastrophic nuclear conflict could be and sought a realistic course to avert it—one who sensed the danger that lurked in a continuing inequality in our land and sought a rational and durable solution—one to whom the phrase "the national interest" was more than a string of words—one who could disagree without vindictiveness—one who believed that the expansion of the enjoyment of living by all people was an achievable goal—one who believed that each generation must contribute its best to the fulfillment of the American dream.

The *Te Deums* which will be sung this day may be wafted away by the evening breeze which caresses the last resting place of those who served the Republic, but here in this chamber where he served and prepared for higher responsibility, the memory of John Fitzgerald Kennedy will long linger to nourish the faith of all who serve that same great land.

Comments in the world press

IT FOUND ITS MARK HERE

"Terrible history has been made in Dallas, and the magnitude of our city's sorrow can only be measured against the enormity of the deed.

"John F. Kennedy, President of the United States of America, is dead. Killed in Dallas. No matter what the explanation of the act, the awful reality of it overwhelms us. He died here.

"We do not know, we may never know, why it happened in Dallas. And it is no comfort to our grief that an insane chance, operating with blind destiny, brought our President's death to us.

"But this we know, that as a city we must show the world the deep unity of our grief, the depths of the stunned void that is in each of us.

"Let us go into the open churches, the cathedrals, the synagogues, and there let us pray to God to teach us love and forgiveness. In the quiet of our homes, let us search our hearts and, through the terrible cleansing power of our grief, remove any vestiges of bitterness and hate.

"What happened here could have happened in any city. But first there had to be the seeds of hate—and we must pray that Dallas can never supply the atmosphere for tragedy to grow again.

"The bullet that felled our President was molded in an unstable world. But to our great sorrow, it found its mark here."

Dallas Times-Herald

A MAN OF HIS GENERATION

"John F. Kennedy was a man of his generation, an eloquent spokesman for that strange new world which the Second War had ushered in. More than any President since Woodrow Wilson, he believed in the power of ideas. His quick intelligence gave him an extraordinary grasp of the vast scope of the Presidential office; his deep intellect molded a philosophy of government that rare oratorical powers enabled him to articulate with grace and with distinction.

"He was a man of the world, who understood the role of the United States in this world. He was a man of peace, who at first hand had experienced war. He was above all a man of political sophistication, who appreciated what the United States could do and what it could not do in its relations abroad. While a brilliant exponent of American democracy, he never fell into the trap of believing in the myth of American omnipotence.

"He was a man of moderation, as he demonstrated repeatedly during his too-brief years in office; he was also a man of courage, as he showed in that moment of acute crisis over Cuba a year ago. . . .

"He has been murderously cut off in the prime of life and power; the Nation has suffered another day of infamy which the American people will never forget."

The New York Times

A SYMBOL OF WARNING

"The assassination charges the American people with a grave responsibility. The martyred President becomes a symbol of warning. Our Democracy is reminded that the very fabric of popular self-government depends upon a universal faith in reason and moderation, in patient accommodation of conflicting views and interests, in the democratic processes of conciliation."

The St. Louis Post-Dispatch

TO BIND UP THE WOUNDS

"The years and the energies of John Kennedy's Presidency were dedicated to an effort to bind up the wounds of his world and his time, to heal the divisions that separate man from man . . . The nation must now face the awesome questions that such a calamity poses.

"Shall we continue to try to heal the wounds of the world? Are we capable of the tolerance and patience and intellect that the search for peace demands? Can we honor the concepts of dignity and decency and brotherhood on which our nation was founded? Or shall we be sacrificed, as our President has been sacrificed, on the altar of man's refusal to live with man?"

The Louisville Courier Journal

THE ONE HERO

"There has never been known such intense world-wide grief as is now felt at President Kennedy's death. Before the assassination one could only half appreciate the weight of responsibility which he carried with such obvious enjoyment and vigour. Now it can be seen clearly that in every country he was a source of confidence and hope, just as much in the world at large as in the West. He was the one authentic hero of the post-war world, and he has been killed."

The Sunday Times, London
November 24, 1963

WHAT IS WRONG?

"It is a national tragedy of incalculable proportions. . . . What is wrong with the United States that it can provide the environment for such an act? There is a sickness in the nation when political differences cannot be accepted and settled in the democratic way."

The St. Louis Post-Dispatch

WE WERE ASHAMED

"There are those of us who, lacking any real knowledge about how much a man must give of himself when he becomes President, voiced bitterness and hatred toward him because we didn't agree with his every act. . . . Friday, we were ashamed there have been so many Americans of that kind."

Charlotte Observer

BROAD OUTLOOK

"The broad outlook of the late President, who realistically assessed the situation and tried to find negotiated solutions for international problems, was highly appreciated in the Soviet Union."

—Izvestia

LAUGHING, SAILING, JOKING

"The pictures that come back are the lively ones: the candidate fighting with a kind of cheerful ferocity for the great office in the performance of whose duties he died; the President laughing, sailing, throwing himself into a speech, joking with his children, reveling in a world full of things to see and hear and think about and, above all, do. Life and color and, to use his favorite word, vigor, went with him everywhere."

The Baltimore Sun

THE FUTURE BETRAYED

"When great men of State die, it is their achievements which come to mind. The tragedy of Kennedy's death is that we have also to mourn the achievements to come. There is a feeling that the future has been betrayed.

"When John Kennedy became President, he not only symbolised youth in a world dominated by older men. He brought with him a sense of intellectual adventure. Suddenly, new prospects seemed possible. Life itself seemed more exciting. He seemed to be not so much the heir to an existing political situation as the herald of a new one. . . .

"It was his style which also gave him his unique personal prestige outside America. His intellectual, somewhat princely, yet keenly professional approach to his tasks had an appeal beyond the shores of America: the sense of excitement which he conveyed quickened the tempo of political life everywhere. He communicated his own sense of adventure to others. Here was a man who saw himself a world leader, heir not only to America's political legacy, but to Europe's intellectual tradition and, through his Irish ancestry, to the hopes and aspirations of underprivileged everywhere. The final irony is that the most rational of present-day statesmen should have met his death as the result of an apparently irrational act.

"In the end, Kennedy's qualities as a man command as much affection as respect. In him, the private man was never lost in the public figure. The friends he made before he became President were the friends he kept while in office. We mourn a man who—with his beautiful wife, his respect for ideas and the arts, his humour, his informality and modesty in the face of the tremendous responsibilities which he fully understood—represented something vital, life-enhancing. His death diminishes us all."

The Observer
November 24, 1963

HE WALKED WITH DIGNITY

"President Kennedy was the patrician dedicating himself to the common man; he was the young man proving that youth is no bar to the Presidency; he was the Catholic proving that a maturing America would close no doors because of a man's faith. He walked into the life he had chosen with dignity. He left that life never having spoiled his office."

Rochester Democrat & Chronicle

A SHARING OF TASKS

"The loss is shared by all, and it must lead to a sharing of the hard tasks ahead. If the death of President Kennedy engenders bitterness among the people he served, we shall betray his sacrifice. If it brings new resolve to meet the challenge together, John F. Kennedy must rest content."

The Washington Star

A STEP FOR EVERY GRUDGING STEP

"In only thirty-four months in office he bore enormous responsibilities in a troubled world and met them with fortitude and hope. It will be recorded of him that he constantly labored to maintain peace in the world, that he was willing to go a step for every grudging step in that direction taken by the Communists, and that he would not permit himself discouragement in his quest to spare the world the searing horror of thermonuclear war."

The Chicago Tribune

A FEELING OF BROTHERHOOD

"An instinctive feeling of brotherhood . . . prompted the high importance he gave to one of the most controversial of his unfinished tasks—the bill for civil rights. By the great majority of Americans, we think, he was sincerely admired and loved."

The New York World-Telegram & Sun

A selection of personal statements

"For three years he and I worked in the closest association. Every few months we met, sometimes on British, sometimes on American soil, and in between interchanged frequent messages and telephone talks. Anyone who knew the President could not fail to realize that behind the captivating charm of manner lay an immense fund of deeply pondered knowledge on a wide range of subjects, political, economic, and military.

"He was one of the best informed statesmen whom it has ever been my lot to meet, but he was altogether without pedantry or any trace of intellectual arrogance. He was very fond of asking questions and trying to find out other people's views. He was chary of giving his own opinion except after much reflection and consideration.

"Admirably briefed as he always was by his staff, he never stuck slavishly to a brief. Unlike some men, with whom discussion is often almost a formality, he was always ready to listen to and be convinced by argument. In this way he brought to the baffling problems of today a remarkable freshness of mind and flexibility of approach, and these were based upon his fundamental moral and mental integrity.

"President Kennedy was a man of the highest physical and moral courage, tested and proved in war and in peace. When things were difficult, almost desperate, he was both resourceful and resolute; and when things seemed a bit easier he displayed a boyish and infectious delight which was irresistible. . . .

"We mourn for him and for his bereaved family, to whom we offer our respectful sympathy, and for the American people. And we mourn him—and this is perhaps the greatest tribute to Jack Kennedy's life and work—for ourselves, for what we and all the world have lost."

> Harold Macmillan,
> former Prime Minister of Great Britain,
> supporting the resolution in the House of Commons.

"President Kennedy yesterday wrote the last and greatest chapter of his *Profiles in Courage*.

"Today, millions of people throughout the world are trying to find words adequate to express their grief and sympathy to his family. The greatest tribute we can pay to his memory is in our everyday lives to do everything we can to reduce the forces of hatred which drive men to do such terrible deeds."

> Richard M. Nixon,
> former Vice President of the United States.

"President Kennedy died as a soldier, under fire, for his duty and in the service of his country. In the name of the French people, a friend at all times of the American people, I salute this great example and this great memory."

> Charles de Gaulle,
> President of France.

"I thought that he was a peace loving, brave and kind man. In fact, all that a man should be. One day I hope that I will follow his example."

> Norman Gerald Shaw, aged 11,
> of King's Sutton, Northamptonshire, England,
> in a letter to Mrs. Kennedy.

"In these tragic hours, all of France is on the side of the United States in its wrath, its sorrow, and also, despite everything, its confidence in the future."

> Georges Pompidou, Premier of France.

We have loved him in life; let us not forget him in death, god bless his family; God bless his wife; Caroline & John Jun: may all the good work he did be carried on; and may the price of his blood of martyrdom bring all men in America more closely together regardless of the colour of one's skin, or breed.

28/11/1963   With the death of President Kennedy every man in the Free World is a Kennedy. His memory would surely inspire hundreds of young men all over the World to take the message. Long live the memory of John Kennedy, the preacher of humanity.

In London, as in other great cities, people came to the American Embassy to write their messages in memory books (left and opposite).

134

"I am deeply grieved by the news of the tragic death of the outstanding statesman, President John Fitzgerald Kennedy of the United States of America.

"The death of J. F. Kennedy is a hard blow to all people who cherish the cause of peace and Soviet-American co-operation.

"The heinous assassination of the United States President at a time when, as a result of the efforts of the peace-loving peoples, there appeared signs of relaxation of international tension and a prospect has opened for improving relations between the U.S.S.R. and the United States, evokes the indignation of Soviet people against the culprits of this base crime.

"I shall remember my personal meetings with President J. F. Kennedy as a person of broad outlook who realistically assessed the situation and tried to find ways for negotiated settlements of the international problems which now divide the world.

"The Soviet Government and the Soviet people share the grief of the American people over this great loss and express the hope that the search for settling disputed questions, a search to which President J. F. Kennedy made a tangible contribution, would be continued in the interests of peace, for the benefit of mankind.

"Accept, Mr. President, my personal condolences."

> Nikita Khrushchev,
> Premier of the Soviet Union,
> in a telegram to President Johnson.

"The loss to the United States and to the world is incalculable. Those who come after Mr. Kennedy must strive the more to achieve the ideals of world peace and human happiness and dignity to which his Presidency was dedicated."

> Sir Winston Churchill,
> former Prime Minister of Great Britain.

"Despite the antagonisms existing between the government of the United States and the Cuban revolution, we have received with profound displeasure the news of the tragic death of President Kennedy.

"All civilized men are always saddened by happenings such as this. Our delegation before the United Nations desires to express that this is the sentiment of the people and of the government of Cuba."

> Carlos Lechuga,
> Cuban Ambassador to the United Nations.

JOHN FITZGERALD KENNEDY

All generous hearts lament the leader killed,
The young chief with the smile, the radiant face,
The winning way that turned a wondrous race
Into sublimer pathways, leading on.

Grant to us Life that though the man be gone
The promise of his spirit be fulfilled.

> John Masefield,
> Poet Laureate of England.

"With his intelligence he had passion—a rare combination. It is passion that moves the world. I think of him in his tremendous stand for civil rights, for the use of the technological resources of this world to feed the hungry, and his deep desire to find a homeland for refugees, irrespective of creed or race. . . . No one can doubt that he has fired the imagination of men in a way that will not be soon forgotten."

> The Venerable Edward Carpenter,
> Archdeacon of Westminster Abbey.

In memory of a great man. "Those whom the gods love die young." May I extend my deepest and heartfelt sympathy to you, Mrs. Kennedy and your children. This is a tragic loss to the cause of peace. He died with his life's work unfinished. We will remember him at the rising and the setting of the sun. May he be commended into God's hands.

R.I.P.

I miss him like I did my father. I shall think of both him & you always and you can be sure that all in Britain think & feel the same. Never has the world been united so much as at this moment.

Never have so much been thought of one man by so many people. God Bless you and the children

Words to remember

Speakers, editorial writers, and cartoonists recalled some of President Kennedy's eloquent words.

A CITY UPON A HILL

. . . No man about to enter high office in this country can ever be unmindful of the contribution which this state has made to our national greatness. Its leaders have shaped our destiny since long before the great Republic was born . . . Its Democratic institutions—including this historic body—have served as beacon-lights for other nations as well as your sister states. For what Pericles said of the Athenians has long been true of this commonwealth:

"We do not imitate—for we are a model to others."

And so it is that I carry with me from this state to that high and lonely office to which I now succeed more than fond memories and firm friendships. The enduring qualities of Massachusetts—the common threads woven by the Pilgrim and the Puritan, the fisherman and the farmer, the Yankee and the immigrant—will not be and could not be forgotten in this nation's executive mansion. They are an indelible part of my life, my conviction, my view of the past, and my hopes for the future.

Allow me to illustrate: During the last sixty days I have been engaged in the task of constructing an administration. It has been a long and deliberate process. Some have counseled greater speed. Others have counseled more expedient tests.

But I have been guided by the standard John Winthrop set before his shipmates on the flagship *Arbella* 331 years ago, as they, too, faced the task of building a new government on a new and perilous frontier.

"We must always consider," he said, "that we shall be as a city upon a hill—the eyes of all people are upon us."

Today, the eyes of all people are truly upon us—and our Government, in every branch, at every level, national, state, and local, must be as a city upon a hill—constructed and inhabited by men aware of their grave trust and their great responsibilities. . . .

Address to the Massachusetts Legislature, January 9, 1961

COURAGE AND SURVIVAL

The message of Cuba, of Laos, of the rising din of Communist voices in Asia and Latin America—these messages are all the same. The complacent, the self-indulgent, the soft societies are about to be swept away with the debris of history. Only the strong, only the industrious, only the determined, only the courageous, only the visionary who determine the real nature of our struggle can possibly survive . . .

Too long we have fixed our eyes on traditional military needs, on armies prepared to cross borders or missiles poised for flight. Now it should be clear that this is no longer enough, that our security may be lost piece by piece, country by country, without the firing of a single missile or the crossing of a single border.

Address to the American Society of Newspaper Editors, April 20, 1961

FREEDOM IS NOT NEGOTIABLE

I hear it said that West Berlin is militarily untenable. And so was Bastogne. And so, in fact, was Stalingrad. Any dangerous spot is tenable if men—brave men—will make it so. . . . We have previously indicated our readiness to remove any actual irritants in West Berlin, but the freedom of that city is not negotiable. We cannot negotiate with those who say, "What's mine is mine and what's yours is negotiable."

Report to the Nation on the Berlin Crisis, July 25, 1961

THE ADAMS FAMILY

First of all, I want to say to Mr. Adams that it is a pleasure to live in your family's old house, and we hope you will come by and see us . . .

I feel that the Adams family intimidates us all, and what it has been, their extraordinary contribution to the public service, I have examined with some care. It is a source of interest to me that this extraordinarily able group of public servants, President Adams and his son, were the only two Presidents of the United States who were not re-elected in the first fifty years of our country's service. So when posterity gives them something better than re-election, it does present a heart-warming thing to some of us who face the hazards of public life.

I think the other quality which I find interesting in the Adamses is their constant dissatisfaction with their own record. . . . In a sense it was their self-love and self-esteem, rather than any rather synthetic sense of their inadequacy, that made them work so hard, and yet made them all feel that they had failed to achieve what they were capable of and what the times demanded.

Remarks upon the publication of the first four volumes of the Adams papers, Washington, D. C., October 3, 1961. (The Mr. Adams addressed in the first sentence was Thomas B. Adams, a great-great-great-grandson of John Adams, and the president of the Massachusetts Historical Association.)

TWITTING THE N.A.M.

. . . I have not always considered the membership of the N.A.M. as among my strongest supporters. I am not sure you have all approached the New Frontier with the greatest possible enthusiasm, and I was therefore somewhat nervous about accepting this invitation, until I did some studying of the history of this organization. I learned that this organization had once denounced on one occasion—I'll quote—"Swollen bureaucracy" as among the triumphs of Karl Marx, and decried on another occasion new governmental "paternalism and socialism." I was comforted when reading this very familiar language to note that I was in very good company. For the first attack I quoted was on Calvin Coolidge and the second on Herbert Hoover.

I remind you of this only to indicate the happy failure of many of our most pessimistic predictions. And that is true of all of us. I recognize that in the last campaign, most of the members of this luncheon group today supported my opponent, except for a very few—who were under the impression that I was my father's son. But I hope that some of your most alarming feelings of a year ago about the imminent collapse of the whole business system if I was elected have been somewhat lessened.

Address to the National Association of Manufacturers, New York City, December 6, 1961

THE WRONG ARGUMENT AT THE WRONG TIME

Some conversations I have heard in our own country sound like old records, long-playing, left over from the middle Thirties.

The debate of the Thirties had its great significance and produced great results but it took place in a different world with different needs and different tasks. . . .

Let us not engage in the wrong argument at the wrong time between the wrong people in the wrong country—while the real problems of our own time grow and multiply, fertilized by our neglect.

> Remarks at the Commencement Exercises,
> Yale University, January 11, 1962

ON THOMAS JEFFERSON

I think this is the most extraordinary collection of talent, of human knowledge, that has ever been gathered together at the White House—with the possible exception of when Thomas Jefferson dined alone.

> Greeting to guests at a White House dinner
> honoring Nobel Prize winners, April 29, 1962

ON DEFIANCE OF LAW

Americans are free to disagree with the law but not to disobey it. For a government of laws and not of men, no man, however prominent and powerful, and no mob, however unruly or boisterous, is entitled to defy a court of law. If this country should ever reach the point where any man or group of men by force or threat of force could long defy the commands of our courts and our Constitution, then no law would stand free from doubt, no judge would be sure of his writ, and no citizen would be safe from his neighbors.

> Remarks to the Nation on the James Meredith case,
> September 30, 1962

OUR COMMON LINK

If we cannot end now our differences, at least we can help make the world safe for diversity. For, in the final analysis, our most basic common link is that we all inhabit this small planet. We all breathe the same air. We all cherish our children's future. And we are all mortal.

Commencement Address, American University, June 11, 1963

IN THE LONG HISTORY OF THE WORLD, ONLY A FEW GENERATIONS HAVE BEEN GRANTED THE ROLE OF DEFENDING FREEDOM IN ITS HOUR OF MAXIMUM DANGER. I DO NOT SHRINK FROM THIS RESPONSIBILITY; I WELCOME IT. I DO NOT BELIEVE THAT ANY OF US WOULD EXCHANGE PLACES WITH ANY OTHER PEOPLE OR ANY OTHER GENERATION. THE ENERGY, THE FAITH, THE DEVOTION WHICH WE BRING TO THIS ENDEAVOR WILL LIGHT OUR COUNTRY AND ALL WHO SERVE IT, AND THE GLOW FROM THAT FIRE CAN TRULY LIGHT THE WORLD.

DAHL IN *The Boston Herald*

CIVIL RIGHTS: A MORAL ISSUE

We are confronted primarily with a moral issue. It is as old as the Scriptures and is as clear as the American Constitution.

The heart of the question is whether all Americans are to be afforded equal rights and equal opportunities, whether we are going to treat our fellow Americans as we want to be treated. If an American, because his skin is dark, cannot eat lunch in a restaurant open to the public, if he cannot send his children to the best public school available, if he cannot vote for the public officials who represent him, if, in short, he cannot enjoy the full and free life which all of us want, then who among us would be content to have the color of his skin changed and stand in his place? Who among us would then be content with the counsels of patience and delay? . . .

> Address to the Nation on civil rights, June 11, 1963

"ICH BIN EIN BERLINER"

Two thousand years ago the proudest boast was "Civitas romanus sum." Today, in the world of freedom, the proudest boast is "Ich bin ein Berliner." (I appreciate my interpreter translating my German.)

There are many people in the world who really don't understand, or say they don't, what is the great issue between the free world and the Communist world. Let them come to Berlin. There are some who say that communism is the wave of the future. Let them come to Berlin. And there are some who say in Europe and elsewhere we can work with the Communists. Let them come to Berlin. And there are even a few who say that it is true that communism is an evil system, but it permits us to make economic progress. "Lasst sie nach Berlin kommen."

Freedom has many difficulties and democracy is not perfect, but we have never had to put a wall up to keep our people in, to prevent them from leaving us. I want to say . . . all free men, wherever they may live, are citizens of Berlin, and, therefore, as a free man, I take pride in the words "Ich bin ein Berliner."

> Remarks upon signing the Golden Book
> in Rudolf Wilde Platz,
> Berlin, Germany, June 26, 1963

TAKING THE FIRST STEP

Yesterday a shaft of light cut into the darkness. Negotiations were concluded in Moscow on a treaty to ban all nuclear tests in the atmosphere, in outer space, and under water. . . .

Now, for the first time in many years, the path of peace may be open. No one can be certain what the future will bring. No one can say whether the time has come for an easing of the struggle. But history and our own conscience will judge us harsher if we do not now make every effort to test our hopes by action, and this is the place to begin. According to the ancient Chinese proverb, "A journey of a thousand miles must begin with a single step."

My fellow Americans, let us take that first step. Let us, if we can, get back from the shadows of war and seek out the way of peace. And if that journey is one thousand miles, or even more, let history record that we, in this land, at this time, took the first step.

> Address to the Nation
> on the Test Ban Treaty, July 26, 1963

Reflections on the man

"GRANDEUR DE KENNEDY"

"History has not created a myth. This man walked undisguised among us, plain, close, and warm, ready to face each day's demands, carrying out his duty as a man to the farthest reaches of the world. . . . He was a runner in a race with fate. He always fought in the open and his meeting with death was face to face. He impressed upon the course of events a spirit of progress that was his own and that leaves us to follow in his footsteps. Servant of a great people dedicated to liberty, and holding high the legacy of his greatest forebears, he was also a soldier of humanity, defender of all rights and all freedoms. No one was more opposed to abstractions than he, nor had a sharper instinct for the heart of a matter: his judgment was both wise and firm, his realism as a statesman was guided as much by humanity as by recognition of the possible. He had that clear, straightforward look of young leaders schooled in friendship. When destiny flings her thunderbolt this high, the tragedy becomes universal and the grief of one people becomes that of all peoples. . . . It is a French flag that I have raised here, to mid-point on the mast of mourning."

Saint-John Perse, winner of the Nobel Award for Literature, in *Le Monde,* November 26, 1963

YOUTH HAS BEEN MOCKED

"I cannot remember a time certainly, in the last thirty years, when the people everywhere around you were so quiet, so tired-looking, and for all their variety of shape and colour and character so plainly the victims of a huge and bitter disappointment. That may sound a queer word to use, but grief is a general term that covers all kinds of sorrow, and I think that what sets off this death from that of other great Americans of our time is the sense that we have been cheated, in a moment—by a wild but devilishly accurate stroke—of the promise of what we had begun to call the Age of Kennedy.

"Let me remind you of a sentence in his Inaugural Address, when he took over the Presidency, on that icy day of January 20, 1961. He said: 'Let the word go forth from this time and place to friend and foe alike that the torch has been passed to a new generation of Americans, born in this century, tempered by war, disciplined by a hard and bitter peace, proud of our ancient heritage and unwilling to witness or permit the slow undoing of those human rights to which this nation has always been committed . . .'

"Of course we knew, older men and women have always known (what in their youth they blithely rattled off as a quotation from Shakespeare) that 'golden lads and girls all must, as chimney sweepers, come to dust.' But it is always stirring to see that young people don't believe it. We chuckled sympathetically then at the warning which Senator Lyndon Johnson had chanted all through the campaign: that the Presidency could not safely be put in the hands of a man 'who has not a touch of gray in his hair.' John Kennedy had turned the tables triumphantly on this argument by saying, in effect, that in a world shivering under the bomb it was the young who had the vigour and the single-mindedness to lead . . .

"It seems to me, looking over the faces of the people and hearing my friends, that the essence of the American mood this very dark weekend is this deep feeling that our youth has been mocked, and the vigour of America for the moment paralyzed . . .

"An American friend from Paris writes: 'I think his death will especially be felt by the young, for he had become for them a symbol of what was possible, with intelligence and will.' An old man, wise in the ups and downs of politics, says: 'I wonder if we knew what he might have grown to in the second term.' A child with wide eyes asks, 'Tell me, will the Peace Corps go on?'

"There is another thing that strikes me, which is allied to the idea of a young lion shot down. It is best seen in the bewilderment of people who were against him, who felt he had temporized and betrayed the promise of the first days. One of them, a politically active woman, rang me up and what she had to say dissolved in tears. Another, a veteran sailor, a close friend and a lifelong Republican, said last night: 'I can't understand, I never felt so close to Kennedy as I do now . . .'

"This charming, complicated, subtle and greatly intelligent man, whom the Western world was proud to call its leader, appeared for a split second in the telescopic sight of a maniac's rifle. And he was snuffed out. In that moment, all the decent grief of a nation was taunted and outraged. So that along with the sorrow, there is a desperate and howling note over the land. We may pray on our knees, but when we get up from them, we cry with the poet:
> 'Do not go gentle into that good night.
> Rage, rage against the dying of the light.'"

Alistair Cooke, *Letter From America* on the BBC, Sunday, November 24, 1963

HE CHALLENGED THE WIND ITSELF

"When we think of him, he is without a hat, standing in the wind and the weather. He was impatient of topcoats and hats, preferring to be exposed, and he was young enough and tough enough to confront and to enjoy the cold and the wind of these times, whether the winds of nature or the winds of political circumstances and national danger. He died of exposure, but in a way that he would have settled for—in the line of duty, and with his friends and enemies all around, supporting him and shooting at him. It can be said of him, as of few men in a like position, that he did not fear the weather, and did not trim his sails, but instead challenged the wind itself, to improve its direction and to cause it to blow more softly and more kindly over the world and its people."

E. B. White
Reprinted by permission; © 1963 *The New Yorker* Magazine, Inc.

The order of the funeral march

District of Columbia police escort.

Escort commander: Major General Philip C. Wehle, Commander of the
     Military District of Washington.

Commander of troops and staff: Lieutenant Colonel Richard E. Cross,
     Commander of the 1st Battalion, 3rd Infantry.

United States Marine Corps Band.

A Company of Military Academy cadets.

A Company of Naval Academy midshipmen.

A Company of Air Force Academy cadets.

A Company of Coast Guard Academy cadets.

A Company of the 1st Battalion, 3rd Infantry, from Fort Myer, Virginia.

A Company of Marines.

A Company of Navy men.

A Squadron from the Air Force.

A Company from the Coast Guard.

A Company of women from the various Armed Services.

The United States Navy Band—heading the second marching unit.

A Company from the Army National Guard.

A Company from the Army Reserves.

A Company from the Marine Corps Reserves.

A Company from the Naval Reserves.

A Squadron from the Air National Guard.

A Squadron from the Air Force Reserves.

A Company from the Coast Guard Reserves.

The United States Air Force Band, heading a third marching unit.

Representatives from the 32 national veterans organizations chartered
     by Congress.

The cortege.

The Special Honor Guard.

A detachment from the Scottish Black Watch.

A detachment from the United States Special Forces at Fort Bragg,
     North Carolina.

A detachment of Marines.

The Joint Chiefs of Staff.

The National Colors.

The clergy.

The horse-drawn caisson.

The President's personal flag.

The riderless horse.

Mrs. Kennedy, President Johnson and Attorney General Robert F. Kennedy.

The Justices of the United States Supreme Court.

The members of the Cabinet.

The members of the Senate and the House of Representatives.

Other mourners.

List of foreign dignitaries who attended the funeral

INTERNATIONAL ORGANIZATIONS

UNITED NATIONS
U Thant, Secretary General
Carlos Sosa Rodriguez, President of the General Assembly
Sir Patrick Dean, President of the Security Council
Dr. Ralph J. Bunche, Under Secretary for Political Affairs
Paul G. Hoffman, Managing Director, Special Fund
Maurice Pate, Executive Director, Children's Fund
David B. Vaughn, Director of General Services
Dr. Louis Alvarado, International Labor Organization
David Blanchard, International Labor Organization

EUROPEAN COAL AND STEEL COMMUNITY
Albert Goppe, Vice President
Jean Monnet, former President

EUROPEAN ECONOMIC COMMUNITY
Jean Rey, Member

EURATOM
E. M. J. A. Sassen. Member of the Council

ORGANIZATION OF AMERICAN STATES
Dr. José A. Mora, Secretary General
Dr. William Sanders, Assistant Secretary General
Rodolfo A. Weidmann, Representative of Argentina
Ilmar Penna Marinho, Representative of Brazil
Don Manuel Trucco, Representative of Chile
Alfredo Jasquez Carrizosa, Representative of Colombia
José Bonilla Atiles, Representative of the Dominican Republic
Dr. Galo Leoro, alternate Representative of Ecuador
Hernan Corrales Padella, Representative of Honduras
Vicente Sanchez Gavito, Representative of Mexico
Andres Fenochio, alternate Representative of Mexico
Dr. Juan Bautista de Lavalle, Representative of Peru
Ward P. Allen, alternate Representative of the United States
Dr. Emilio N. Oribe, interim Representative of Uruguay

EUROPE

AUSTRIA
Alfons Gorbach, Chancellor

BELGIUM
Baudouin I, King of the Belgians
Paul-Henri Spaak, Foreign Minister

BULGARIA
Miliko Tarabanov, Deputy Foreign Minister

CZECHOSLOVAKIA
Dr. Jiri Hajek, Permanent Representative at the United Nations

DENMARK
Crown Prince George
Jens Krag, Premier

FINLAND
Vali Merikoski, Foreign Minister
Max Jacobson, Political Director, Ministry of Foreign Affairs

FRANCE
General Charles de Gaulle, President
Maurice Couve de Murville, Foreign Minister
Etienne Burin des Roziers, Secretary General of the Presidency
General Charles Ailleret, Chairman, Joint Chiefs of Staff

WEST GERMANY
Dr. Heinrich Lübke, President
Dr. Ludwig Erhard, Chancellor
Dr. Gerhard Schröder, Foreign Minister
Kai-Uwe von Hassel, Defense Minister
Willy Brandt, Mayor of West Berlin

GREAT BRITAIN
Prince Philip, Duke of Edinburgh
Sir Alec Douglas-Home, Prime Minister
Harold Wilson, Leader of the Labor party
Jo Grimond, Leader of the Liberal party

GREECE
Frederika, Queen of the Hellenes
Sophocles Venizelos, Deputy Premier and Foreign Minister

HUNGARY
Peter Moj, First Deputy Foreign Minister
Karoly Csatorday, Representative at the United Nations

ICELAND
Gudmundur I. Gudmundson, Foreign Minister

IRELAND
Dr. Eamon de Valera, President
Frank Aiken, Minister for External Affairs
Major Vivian de Valera

ITALY
Cesare Merzagora, President of the Senate
Attilio Piccioni, Foreign Minister
Piero Vinci, Chef de Cabinet, Foreign Ministry
Guerino Roberti, Assistant Chief of Protocol
General Emiliano Scotti, Military Counselor to the President

LUXEMBOURG
Prince Jean, Hereditary Grand Duke
Eugene Schaus, Foreign Minister

THE NETHERLANDS
Prince Bernhard, Consort of the Queen
Crown Princess Beatrix
J. M. A. H. Luns, Foreign Minister

NORWAY
Crown Prince Harald
Einer Gerhardsen, Premier

POLAND
Professor Stanislaw Kulczynski, Deputy Chairman of the Council of State
Piotr Jaroszewicz, Deputy Premier

PORTUGAL
Luis Supico Pinto, President of the Corporate Chamber
General Jose Ponte Rodrigues

RUMANIA
Gheorghe Gaston Marin, Vice President of the Council of Ministers
M. Milita, Deputy Foreign Minister
Victor Ionescu, Minister of Foreign Trade
Vasile Pungan, Director of North American Affairs

SPAIN
General Augustin Muñoz Grandes, Vice Premier
Admiral Pedro Nieto, Naval Minister

SWEDEN
Prince Bertil
Tage Erlander, Premier
Olaf Palme, Minister Without Portfolio

SWITZERLAND
Dr. Friedrich T. Wahlen, Chief of the Federal Political Department
Pierre Micheli, Secretary General of the Federal Political Department

TURKEY
Ismet Inonu, Premier
Feridun Cemal Erkin, Foreign Minister

U.S.S.R.
Anastas I. Mikoyan, First Deputy Premier
Anatoly F. Dobrynin, Ambassador to the United States
Mikhail Smirnovsky, Chief, American Section, Ministry of Foreign Affairs

YUGOSLAVIA
Koca Popovic, Foreign Minister
Petar Stambolic, President of the Federal Executive Council

THE VATICAN
The Most Reverend Egidio Vagnozzi, Archbishop of Myra, Apostolic Delegate

ASIA

CAMBODIA *
Prince Norodom Kantol, President of the Council of Ministers
Chan Youran, Director of Political Affairs, Ministry of Foreign Affairs

CHINA
Tingfu F. Tsiang, Ambassador to the United States

CYPRUS
Zenon Rossides, Ambassador to the United States

INDIA
Mrs. Vijaya Lakshmi Pandit, Delegate to the United Nations

INDONESIA
General Abdul Haris Nasution, Minister for Defense and Security Affairs
Dr. Subjarwo Tjondronegoro, Deputy Foreign Minister

IRAN
Shaphur Gholam Reza
Abbas Aram, Foreign Minister

IRAQ
Ali Haidar Sulaiman, Ambassador to the United States

ISRAEL
Zalman Shazar, President
Mrs. Golda Meir, Foreign Minister

JAPAN
Hayato Ikeda, Premier
Masayoshi Ohira, Foreign Minister

JORDAN
Antone Atallah, Foreign Minister

KOREA
Chung Hee Park, President
Yong Shik Kim, Foreign Minister
Chung Hoy Kim, Ambassador to the United States

LAOS
Tiao Khampan, Ambassador to the United States
Sisouk Na Champassak, Ambassador to India

LEBANON
Ibrahim Ahdab, Ambassador to the United States
George Hakim, Representative at the United Nations

NEPAL
M. P. Koirala, Ambassador to the United States
PAKISTAN
Zulfiqar Ali Bhutto, Foreign Minister
THE PHILIPPINES
Diosdado Macapagal, President
Amelito Mutuc, Ambassador to the
United States
Senator Raul Manglapus
SAUDI ARABIA
Rashad Pharaon, Ambassador to France
Abdullah Hababi, Chargé d'Affaires in
Washington
SYRIA
Salah Al-Din Tarazi, Ambassador to the
United Nations
Walid Majid, Chargé d'Affaires in Washington
Jawdat el Mufti, Minister to the United Nations
THAILAND
Thanat Khouman, Foreign Minister
Sukit Nimanheim, Ambassador-designate
VIETNAM
Tran Chanh Thanh, Ambassador-designate
YEMEN
Muhsin al-Ayni, Ambassador to the
United States

AUSTRALIA AND NEW ZEALAND

AUSTRALIA
Sir Alexander McMullin, President of the Senate
NEW ZEALAND
George R. Laking, Ambassador to the
United States

WESTERN HEMISPHERE

ARGENTINA
Carlos Humberto Perette, Vice President
Dr. Miguel Angel Zavala Ortiz, Foreign Minister
Brigadier Ignacio Avalos, Secretary of War
BAHAMAS
Sir Roland Symonette, Premier-designate
BOLIVIA
Enrique Sanchez Delozada, Ambassador to the
United States
BRAZIL
Senator Auro Moura Andrade, President of
the Senate
João Augusto de Araujo Castro,
Foreign Minister
Roberto de Oliveira Campos, Ambassador to the
United States
Senator Zitorino Freire, Majority Leader
Senator Antonio Carlos Konder Reis,
Minority Leader
CANADA
Lester B. Pearson, Prime Minister
Paul Martin, External Affairs Minister
CHILE
Carlos Martinez, Representative at the
United Nations
COLOMBIA
Alberto Lleras Camargo, former President
German Zea, Ambassador to the United States
COSTA RICA
José Figueres, former President
ECUADOR
Dr. Neftali Ponce Miranda, Foreign Minister
EL SALVADOR
Dr. Hector Escobar Serrano, Foreign Minister

GUATEMALA
Alberto Herrarte Gonzalez, Foreign Minister
José de Dios Augilar, Private Secretary to the
Government
HAITI
Carlet Auguste, Ambassador to the
United Nations
Fern Baguidy, Ambassador to the Organization
of American States
JAMAICA
Sir Alexander Bustamante, Prime Minister
Brigadier Paul Cook, Chief of Staff
James Lloyd, Permanent Secretary, External
Affairs Ministry
Noël Croswell, Commissioner of Police
MEXICO
Manuel Tello, Foreign Minister
NICARAGUA
Luis Somoza de Bayle, Senator and former
President
Dr. Alfonso Ortega Urbina, Foreign Minister
PANAMA
Galileo Solis, Foreign Minister
Arturo Morgan Morales, of the Foreign Ministry
PARAGUAY
Dr. Jan Plate, Ambassador to the United States
PERU
Dr. Victor Andres Belaunde, Representative
at the United Nations
TRINIDAD AND TOBAGO
Sir Ellis E. I. Clarke, Ambassador to the
United States
URUGUAY
Juan Felipe Yriart, Ambassador to the
United States
VENEZUELA
Runaldo Leandro Mora, Acting Foreign
Minister
General Antonio Briceño Linares,
Defense Minister

AFRICA

ALGERIA
Abdelkadir Chanderli, Representative at the
United Nations
Haj Ben Alla, President of the
National Assembly
Amai Ouzegane, Minister of State
Cherif Guellal, Ambassador to the United States
Abdelazziz Bouteflika, Foreign Minister
Laiashi Vaker, Director of Economic Affairs,
Ministry of Foreign Affairs
BURUNDI
Leon Ndenzako, Ambassador to the
United States
CAMEROON *
Benoit Balla-Ondoux, Foreign Minister
CONGO (*Brazzaville*)
E. D. Dadet, Ambassador to the United States
CONGO (*Leopoldville*)
Jacques Masangu, Deputy Premier
ETHIOPIA
Haile Selassie I, Emperor
Ras Andare Atchew Massai
Commander Iskander Desta
Tefara-Woro Kidane-Wold
Lij Kassa Wolde-Mariam
GHANA
Miguel A. Ribeiro, Ambassador to the
United States

K. Armah, High Commissioner in London
Alex Quaison-Sackey, Representative at the
United Nations
GUINEA *
Saifonlaye Diallo, Minister of State
Leon Maka, President of the National Assembly
Alessane Dion, Minister of Communications
IVORY COAST *
Phillipe Yace, President of the National
Assembly
Camille Alliali, Minister Delegate for
Foreign Affairs
Konan Bedie, Ambassador to the United States
LIBERIA
William A. Tolbert, Vice President
J. Rudolph Grimes, Secretary of State
LIBYA
Dr. Wahbi Elbouri, Representative at the
United Nations
MALAGASY REPUBLIC
Louis Rakotomalela, Ambassador to the
United States
MALI
Oumar Sow, Ambassador to the United States
Sory Coulibaly, Ambassador to the
United Nations
Boubacar Casse, Deputy Secretary General,
Ministry of Foreign Affairs
MOROCCO
Prince Moulay Abdullah
Ahmed Reda Guedira, Foreign Minister
Abdelkadar Benjelloun, Minister of Justice
Ali Benjelloun, Ambassador to the United States
Ahmed Taibi Benhima, Representative at the
United Nations
Badir Din Senoussi, Attaché to the
Royal Cabinet
Mohammed Ziani, Attaché to the Cabinet of
the Foreign Minister
General Mohammed Ameziane, Inspector
General of the Royal Armed Forces
Colonel Moulay Hafid, Director General of
Royal Protocol
SENEGAL
Dr. Ousmane Soce Diop, Ambassador to the
United States
SIERRA LEONE
Dr. John Karefa-Smart, Minister of
External Affairs
SOMALIA
Mohammed Ali Daar, Under Secretary for
Foreign Affairs
SOUTH AFRICA
Dr. Willem C. Naude, Ambassador to the
United States
TANGANYIKA
Chief Erasto A. M. Mangyenya, Representative
at the United Nations
TUNISIA
Bahi Ladgham, Secretary of State for
the Presidency
Mongi Slim, Foreign Minister
Taieb Slim, Representative at the United Nations
Habib Bourguiba, Jr.
Hachmi Quanes
UGANDA
Apollo K. Kironde, Representative at the
United Nations
UNITED ARAB REPUBLIC
Mahmond Fawsi, Foreign Minister
Mahmud Riad, Ambassador to the
United Nations

---

* The delegates from Cambodia, Cameroon, Guinea, and Ivory Coast arrived
too late for the funeral but attended President Johnson's reception.

The funeral eulogy

Given in St. Matthew's Church by the Most Reverend Philip M. Hannan, Auxiliary Bishop of Washington.

Mrs. Kennedy and children, beloved mother and members of the family, the President of the United States, your Majesties and distinguished heads of government, representatives of the distinguished heads of state, your Eminence Cardinal Cushing, your Excellency, the Most Reverend Representative of the Holy Father, your Excellency the Archbishop and Bishops, Monsignor Cartwright, your Excellencies, the Ambassadors, the Speaker of the House, distinguished members of the judiciary, the Congress, the Government, and distinguished friends all of President John Fitzgerald Kennedy:

It was thought that the most appropriate commemoration of this heartbreaking event would be the expression of President John Fitzgerald Kennedy's ideals and sources of inspiration in his own words.

President John Kennedy was fond of quoting the Holy Bible. At the last dinner of his life in Houston, Texas, last Thursday night, he applied to a friend, as it should be applied to him, this combination of passages from the Proverbs and the prophecy of Joel: "Your old men shall dream dreams, your young men shall see visions, and where there is no vision the people perish."

And to those who shared his vision in this land and abroad he had said two months ago to the United Nations:

"Let us complete what we have started, for as the Scriptures tell us, no man who puts his hand to the plow and looks back is fit for the kingdom of God."

At this time of sorrow and burden, he would have us remember the passages from Joshua and Isaiah he had used in accepting the presidential nomination: "Be strong and of good courage. Be not afraid, neither be thou dismayed. They that wait upon the Lord shall renew their strength. They shall mount up with wings as eagles. They shall run and not be weary."

Finally, in his last hours, President Kennedy had prepared these words for Dallas and for the nation:

"The righteousness of our cause must always underlie our strength, for as was written long ago, except the Lord guard the city, the guard watches in vain."

The following is one of his favorite passages from Scripture, from the Book of Ecclesiastes, the third chapter:

"There is an appointed time for everything, and a time for every affair under the heavens.

"A time to be born, and a time to die. A time to plant, and a time to uproot the plant.

"A time to kill, and a time to heal. A time to tear down, and a time to build.

"A time to weep, and a time to laugh. A time to mourn, and a time to dance.

"A time to scatter stones, and a time to gather them. A time to embrace, and a time to be far from embraces.

"A time to seek, and a time to lose. A time to keep, and a time to cast away.

"A time to rend, and a time to sew. A time to be silent, and a time to speak.

"A time to love, and a time to hate. A time of war, and a time of peace."

And now is the final expression of his ideals and aspirations—from his Inaugural Address:

"We observe today not a victory of party but a celebration of freedom—symbolizing an end as well as a beginning—signifying renewal as well as change.

"Let the word go forth from this time and place, to friends and foe alike, that the torch has been passed to a new generation of Americans—born in this century, tempered by war, disciplined by a hard and bitter peace, proud of their ancient heritage—and unwilling to witness or permit the slow undoing of those human rights to which this nation has always been committed, and to which we are committed today at home and around the world.

"Let every nation know, whether it wishes us well or ill, that we shall pay any price, bear any burden, meet any hardship, support any friend, oppose any foe to assure the survival and the success of liberty.

"Let both sides unite to heed in all corners of the earth the command of Isaiah—'to undo the heavy burdens . . . and let the oppressed go free.'

"All this will not be finished in the first 100 days, nor will it be finished in the first 1,000 days, nor in the life of this Administration, nor even perhaps in our lifetime on this planet.

"But let us begin. In your hands, my fellow citizens, more than mine, will rest the final success or failure of our course.

"Since this country was founded, each generation of Americans has been summoned to give testimony to its national loyalty.

"The graves of young Americans who answered the call to service surround the globe. Now the trumpet summons us again —not as a call to bear arms, though arms we need, not as a call to battle, though embattled we are—but a call to bear the burden of a long twilight struggle year in and year out, 'rejoicing in hope, patient in tribulation'—a struggle against the common enemies of man: tyranny, poverty, disease and war itself.

"In the long history of the world, only a few generations have been granted the role of defending freedom in its hour of maximum danger.

"I do not shrink from this responsibility—I welcome it. I do not believe that any of us would exchange places with any other people or any other generation.

"The energy, the faith, the devotion which we bring to this endeavor will light our country and all who serve it—and the glow from that fire can truly light the world.

"And so, my fellow Americans, ask not what your country can do for you, ask what you can do for your country.

"With a good conscience our only sure reward, with history the final judge of our deeds, let us go forth to lead the land we love, asking His blessing and His help but knowing that here on earth God's work must truly be our own."

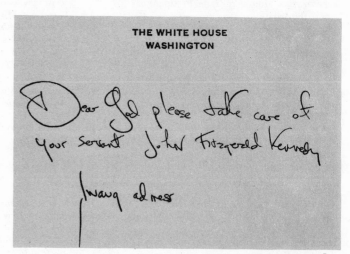

Mrs. Kennedy's hand-written instructions for the funeral card at the church. Her own words were followed by a quotation from the Inaugural Address.

The prayer at the grave

Spoken by Richard Cardinal Cushing, Archbishop of Boston,
at the President's grave. (Some words were inaudible.)

In the name of the Father and of the Son and of the Holy Ghost. Amen.
Let us pray.

O God, through whose mercy the souls of the faithful find rest, be pleased
to bless this grave and Thy holy angels to keep it . . . the body we bury
herein, that of our beloved Jack Kennedy, the 35th President of the United
States, that his soul may rejoice in Thee with all the saints, through Christ
our Lord. Amen.

I am the resurrection and the life. Blessed be the Lord God of Israel because He hath visited and wrought redemption to His people and had raised
up a horn of salvation to us in the House of David, His servant, as He
[spoke through] His holy prophets of old from the beginning. Salvation
from our enemies and from the hand of all who hate us. Show mercy to our
fathers and to remember His holy covenants.

The oath which He swore to Abraham our father that He would grant
unto us, that being delivered from the hand of our enemies we may serve
Him without fear. Holiness and justice also before Him all our days. Thy
child shall be called the prophet of the Most High for thou shalt go before
the face of the Lord to prepare His way.

To give knowledge of salvation to his people unto the remission of their
sins. Because of the mercy of God in which the . . . from on high has
visited us.

To enlighten them that sit in darkness and in the shadow of death to
direct our feet into the way of peace.

Eternal rest grant unto him, O Lord, and let perpetual light shine upon
him.

I am the resurrection and the life. He who believeth in Me, although
he be dead, shall live, and everyone who liveth and believeth in Me, shall
not die forever.

Lord have mercy on us. Christ have mercy on us, God have mercy on us.

Our Father, Who art in heaven, hallowed be Thy name. Thy kingdom
come, Thy will be done on earth, as it is in heaven.

Give us this day our daily bread, and forgive us our trespasses as we forgive those who trespass against us. And lead us not into temptation, but
deliver us from evil. Amen.

From the gates of hell, deliver his soul, O Lord, that he may rest in
peace. Amen.

O Lord, hear my prayer and let my cry come unto Thee.

The Lord be with you and with thy spirit.

Let us pray:

Grant, O Lord, this mercy to Thy servant departed, that he who in his
desires did Thy will may not receive the punishment of any misdeeds, and
that as through faith that joined him to the company of the faithful here
below, Thy mercy may make him the companion of the holy angels in
heaven, through Christ our Lord. Amen.

A NOTE ON THIS BOOK

This book was produced jointly by United Press International and the American Heritage Publishing Co., Inc.

For American Heritage: Richard M. Ketchum, Editor of the Book Division; Irwin Glusker, Art Director. For United Press International: Earl J. Johnson, Editor and Vice President; Harold Blumenfeld, Executive Newspictures Editor.

The photographs are from the UPI newspicture services. The sequences showing the assassination of the President and the shooting of Oswald are from UPI Newsfilm. The picture on pages 88–89 is copyright, 1963, by Bob Jackson and the *Dallas Times-Herald*.

Library of Congress Catalogue Card Number: 64–15726